To Jaq

AT THE END OF THE ROAD, TURN EAST,
AND YOU SHOULD FIND THE COURTS. (5)

When you can open this book, understand, and solve the clue above,
you no longer need

How to Solve Cryptic Crosswords.

HOW TO SOLVE CRYPTIC CROSSWORDS

Kevin Skinner

RIGHT WAY

Constable & Robinson Ltd
3 The Lanchesters
162 Fulham Palace Road
London W6 9ER
www.right-way.co.uk
www.constablerobinson.com

First published in the UK 1993

This edition published by Right Way, an imprint of
Constable & Robinson, 2008

A copy of the British Library Cataloguing in Publication
Data is available from the British Library

ISBN: 978-0-7160-2208-4

Printed and bound in the EU

CONTENTS

INTRODUCTION

For many years I have been a great devotee of the crossword, as of course have many millions of others. Exactly when I discovered the Cryptic Crossword I cannot recall, but it was totally beyond my comprehension how anyone could extract an answer from the seemingly nonsensical clues given.

In an effort to discover this cipher-cracking ability, and to become proficient at it, I became a regular reader (not the correct description as I bought it primarily for the crossword) of a daily paper that featured a relatively easy one. As one would expect, I did, gradually, over a period of many months/years, develop an understanding of the logic or reasoning behind the clues and now enjoy the challenge of the many, varying degrees of difficulty, cryptic crosswords which are available in virtually every newspaper. Contrary to popular belief, one does not have to be exceptionally intelligent to understand and enjoy them: I have a friend who certainly wouldn't make a quiz team, yet has an amazing grasp of the Cryptic clue.

Once the skill has been established, it is, in my opinion, easier to arrive at the correct answer with a Cryptic clue than a Straight clue, thereby avoiding ugly alterations. The reason for this is that not only is one frequently given a 'straight' clue, but also a further clue to 'cross refer' as it were. I will demonstrate.

A straight clue may read;

12 Down   FISH (5).

Now as you will agree, there are many, many fish with names comprising of five letters. How can one establish which particular variety is the required answer? One can't, so one must try to solve other answers in order to match crossing letters in the crossword grid. This is not foolproof, as there are many words with similar letter patterns, e.g. pErCH or tEnCH. The error is then discovered later, which means having to make untidy corrections.

Alternatively, a Cryptic clue may read;

BIRDS SIT ON THIS FISH. (5)

Now accepting that my ornithological knowledge is somewhat limited, I don't think that any bird sits on a Tench or a Bream, which leads us to the logical answer which, as you have probably guessed, is a PERCH.

This is a relatively simple example, let's find out more about the Cryptic Clue.

PART ONE
LEARNING

1

THE CRYPTIC CLUE
IN GENERAL

What does Cryptic actually mean?

The definition of the word Cryptic, is 'obscure' or 'secret'. The opposite of cryptic is 'obvious'. This is very important to remember, as in cryptic crossword clues, what would appear to be obvious is in fact quite the reverse.

What is a Cryptic Clue?

A Cryptic clue is a sentence of varying length that is in fact a string of assorted 'types' of clue i.e. Anagrams, Double Straight, Abbreviations etc. Each individual clue, when solved, produces a word, or letter, that contributes to the required answer.

How does one recognize these 'types' of clues?

Each different clue usually has an 'indicating' word or pointer to signify its use. The learning of these indicating words and pointers is the purpose of this book, and normally is a skill that takes many months/years to acquire, but with this book that time will be dramatically reduced!

As we progress, you will learn to recognize and have the opportunity to practise the various clues and indicating words with small 'tester' crosswords.

How does one separate the clues within the clues?

Possibly the most important element of solving cryptic crosswords, and should be regarded as the first lesson, is the technique of inserting the mental comma.

A chemist has the expertise to look at a complex chemical formula and recognize it as simply a cough medicine. With the insertion of one, two or even three mental commas, one can, like the chemist, look at a clue sentence and see it as a 'formula' of different clues.

The importance of a comma cannot be underestimated, whether one is writing a letter, or solving a cryptic crossword. This is demonstrated in the following sentence "MARY QUEEN OF SCOTS WALKED THE BLOODY TOWER TEN MINUTES AFTER HER HEAD WAS CUT OFF." Without commas being inserted the sentence is quite bizarre, but with the introduction of two commas, after the words *tower* and *after*, the sentence becomes logical and reasonable (not that Her Highness would have agreed).

2

DOUBLE STRAIGHT CLUES

It is the ability to insert mental commas that allows the cryptic crossworder to decipher, or 'break down', the clue sentences.

An example of the importance of the "mental" comma is demonstrated in the clue given in the introduction earlier.

BIRDS SIT ON THIS FISH. (5)

Introducing a comma after the word 'this', to denote the end of a clue, suddenly makes two straight clues;

BIRDS SIT ON THIS / FISH.

You will agree that what was a difficult clue, requiring a visit to the library for reference, is now very simple to answer. I call this particular type of clue a 'Double Straight' clue and it is the first type of clue I look for.

Let's look at more examples of the Double Straight.

TENDS TO WORK IN HOSPITALS (6)

A straight clue may read TENDS, or even TO WORK IN HOSPITALS.

A six letter word that accommodates both the straight clues is, as you've probably guessed, NURSES.

A PART TIME COPPER IS CLOSE TO ME (7)

(Insert comma between A PART TIME COPPER / IS CLOSE TO ME.) A part time copper is a SPECIAL, and is close to me is SPECIAL. Answer = SPECIAL

STAYS FOR THE LEFT-OVERS. (7)

(Insert comma between STAYS FOR / THE LEFT-OVERS.) Someone who stays for REMAINS and so are LEFT-OVERS. Answer = REMAINS

CLIMBS WEIGHING MACHINE (6)

(Insert comma between CLIMBS / WEIGHING MACHINE.) To climb is to SCALE as is a weighing machine. Answer = SCALES

MAKE A TELEPHONE CALL FOR THE BOXER TO MOVE IN (4)
(Comma inserted between CALL / FOR). Answer = RING

Now try two small Double Straight Crosswords for yourself.

3

DOUBLE STRAIGHT CLUE
CROSSWORDS

No. 1

ACROSS
(1) Weight of money. (6)
(5) Normal type of blonde. (7)
(6) Led on by pulling leg. (6)

DOWN
(1) Smooth wood flying machine. (5)
(2) Outdo someone in front of the audience. (7)
(3) Got qualifications bit by bit. (7)
(4) Combine a mix of coffee. (5)

No. 2

ACROSS
(1) Result of losing one's temper with a seal. (5)
(3) Watch end of needle. (3)
(6) Homesteader is a payer of the money owed. (7)
(7) This old horse will go on and on and on. (3)
(8) Lessened pain by slackening joint. (5)

DOWN
(1) Time of the year to use salt and pepper maybe. (6)
(2) What one does with too much sun and potatoes. (5)
(4) Deserved to get money for working. (6)
(5) Old coach to act on. (5)

Answers to Double Straight Clue Crosswords

As one is given two straight clues no further explanation is necessary other than to indicate where the imaginary comma should have been inserted. A ' / ' shows this.

No. 1
ACROSS
(1) Weight / of money........................ Ans: POUNDS

(5) Normal / type of blonde.................. Ans: NATURAL

(6) Led on / by pulling leg.................. Ans: TEASED

DOWN
(1) Smooth wood / flying machine............. Ans: PLANE

(2) Outdo someone / in front of the audience.... Ans: UPSTAGE

(3) Got qualifications / bit by bit.............. Ans: DEGREES

(4) Combine / a mix of coffee................ Ans: BLEND

No. 2
ACROSS
(1) Result of losing one's temper / with a seal... Ans: STAMP

(3) Watch / end of needle.................... Ans: EYE

(6) Homesteader / is a payer of money owed.... Ans: SETTLER

(7) This old horse / will go on and on and on... Ans: NAG

(8) Lessened pain / by slackening joint......... Ans: EASED

DOWN
(1) Time of the year / to use salt and
pepper maybe.......................... Ans: SEASON

(2) What one does with too much sun / and
potatoes .... Ans: PEELS

(4) Deserved / to get money for working....... Ans: EARNED

(5) Old coach / to act on.................... Ans: STAGE

The 'double straight' is always the first type of clue to look for. It is quite common, relatively easy to solve, and quickly recognisable.

4

THE ANAGRAM

With the exception of the Single Cryptic clue, which we shall advance to later, one should expect to find at least one straight clue in the overall clue sentence. THIS WILL ALWAYS BE THE OPENING WORD/S, or CLOSING WORD/S of the sentence. It will either be preceded or succeeded by one of the other types of clue which we shall be learning as we progress through this book. The straight clue should never be in the middle of the clue sentence. Were it to be, it would be bad compiling.

In the examples in this section I shall make the 'balance' of the clues anagrams.

An anagram is a given word (or words) which, when its letters are transposed, makes another word (or words). For our purposes, it means to mix up the section of the clue we are given to make a new word, which will then reveal our answer, or contribute towards the answer. But, before we proceed I must explain how to recognize that it is in fact an anagram.

The secret is in the two words *mix up*, which is an anagram indicator. What it is actually saying is "re-order" or "move around". Any word that suggests this can indicate the anagram, e.g. jumble, mess, crazy, mad, upset. These are relatively obvious. Many other words will be used by the compiler to allow the whole clue sentence to 'flow' and cleverly conceal the anagram indicator. E.g.

I TRIED TO BE ORGANISED AND NEATER (6)
Using the mental comma, I TRIED / TO BE ORGANISED (Anagram indicator) / AND NEATER (straight Clue).
The answer of course is TIDIER.
Further examples follow. (Anagram Indicator in italics, (/) = mental comma, Straight clue marked (Str.).)

ARRANGE / LEASE / FOR THE ARTIST (Str.) (5)........ Ans: EASEL

UNUSUALLY / REMOTE / SHOOTING STAR (Str.) (6)... Ans: METEOR

CATERER / *WAS PREPARED* / TO GO BACK OVER (Str.) (7)
....Ans: RETRACE

IT WOULD BE A SINGULAR ADVANTAGE (Str.) / *TO RESHAPE* / HARD TIN
BEHIND (4,2,3,4)................... Ans: BIRD IN THE HAND

There are of course hundreds of words that can indicate an anagram
but I have listed below the most commonly used.

A	Concealing	F	L
Abnormal	Confuse	False	Lousy
About	Construction	Fashioned	
Adapt	Convert	Fixed	M
Adjust	Correct	Funny	Mad
Affect	Crooked		Made
Agitate	Curious	G	Manipulate
Anyway		Gives	Manoeuvre
Around	D	Goes	Maybe
Astray	Deception	Gyrate	Messy
Awful	Defected		Mince
Awkward	Deranged		Mix
	Design	H	Model
B	Develop	Havoc	Modify
Bad	Devious	Haywire	Molested
Becomes	Devised	Horrible	Mould
Bent	Different		Muddled
Break	Disperse	I	Mysterious
Brew	Divert	Impaired	
Broken	Doctor	Incorrect	N
Bust	Drunk	Insane	New
	Dubious	Irritated	
C			O
Careless		J	Obscure
Change	E	Juggled	Odd
Chaos	Effect		Ordered
Circling	Emend		Organised
Cocktail	Engineered	K	Out
Compose	Erratic	Kind of	Over

P	Resolved	Silly	Turned
Peculiar	Reviewed	Sorry	Twisted
Placed	Revolving	Sort	
Positioned	Roving	Spoiled	U-W
Possibly	Re-worded	Stir	Untie
Prepared		Strange	Unusual
Processed			Upset
Put Out			Use
	S		Variety
Q	Scramble	T	Vary
Queer	Serve up	Terrible	Wandering
	Set	Tip	Way
	Shambles	Transform	Weird
R	Shift	Translate	Wild
Repaired	Shuffled	Trick	Wrong

Many of the above words may have the 'ED' extension, e.g. ADAPT ADAPTED, CORRECT CORRECTED. Always be vigilant for anagram indicators as they are always there in varying abundance.

5

MAKING NOTES

During the process of solving Cryptic Clues, it is essential to make notes as the clue is read.

As explained earlier, when one inserts an imaginary comma, the preceding word or words indicate a letter, or string of letters. As these gradually emerge, make a note of them and the answer will unfold as it is written (well....often), e.g.

MAKE A POINT TO WARM THE CEREAL (5)

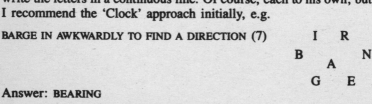

Answer: W-HEAT or WHEAT

Cryptic Crosswords usually include at least a couple of Anagrams, more often several. Sometimes (in my opinion to the crossword's detriment) very many.

Once it is realized that a particular word (or words) is an Anagram, I find the easiest way to 'see' the word required is to write down the letters in a 'Clock' format. That is to say, a rim of letters with a key letter (preferably a vowel) in the centre. This, I must stress, is a personal preference. I do know of people who prefer to write the letters in a continuous line. Of course, each to his own, but I recommend the 'Clock' approach initially, e.g.

BARGE IN AWKWARDLY TO FIND A DIRECTION (7)

Answer: BEARING

(Yet another Anagram indicator, AWKWARDLY.) It is virtually impossible to solve an Anagram without writing down the letters, but it is rare to find a space that is designated for note-making in newspapers as blank areas are costly. For this reason I leave plenty of room for note making by the crosswords in this book.

6
ANAGRAM CROSSWORDS

No. 1

ACROSS
(1) Sue sit around and blow your nose in this. (6)
(4) Strange a sawn dam. (5)
(7) Untie laces to climb. (5)
(9) C.I.D. Dan turned honest. (6)

DOWN
(1) A side of mixed meat. (4)
(2) Maybe was a cutter. (3)
(3) Run about to get pot. (3)
(5) Car goes round and round. (3)
(6) Over dale and out front. (4)
(7) Pa's been put out to water. (3)
(8) Dan is going also. (3)

No. 2

ACROSS
(1) To do this would upset teach. (5)
(3) Lee messed around with fish. (3)
(6) Largely confused with a rash. (7)
(7) Tea is used for this application. (3)
(8) Nigel used marbles. (5)

DOWN
(1) Pea can be made into an appetizer. (6)
(2) Rates make me bring these to my eyes. (5)
(4) A manly sort but still a novice. (6)
(5) Petal serves up my dinner on it. (5)

Answers to Anagram Crosswords

Words in italics are the words that 'indicate' the Anagram. The actual Anagram is followed by (Anag), and the 'Straight' clue is followed by (Str).

No. 1
ACROSS

(1) Sue sit (Anag) *around* and blow your nose in this (Str) ....Ans: TISSUE

(4) *Strange* a sawn (Anag) dam (Str).............Ans: ASWAN

(7) *Untie* laces (Anag) to climb (Str).............Ans: SCALE

(9) C.I.D. Dan (Anag) *turned* honest (Str).......Ans: CANDID

DOWN

(1) A side (Str) of *mixed* meat (Anag).............Ans: TEAM

(2) *Maybe* was (Anag) a cutter (Str)................Ans: SAW

(3) Run (Anag) *about* to get pot (Str)..............Ans: URN

(5) Car (Anag) *goes round* and round (Str).........Ans: ARC

(6) *Over* dale (Anag) and out front (Str)...........Ans: LEAD

(7) Pa's (Anag) *been put out* to water (Str)...........Ans: SPA

(8) Dan (Anag) *is going* also (Str)................Ans: AND

No. 2
ACROSS

(1) To do this would *upset* teach (Anag) (All words Str).......
Ans: CHEAT

(3) Lee (Anag) *messed around* with fish (Str)........Ans: EEL

(6) Largely (Anag) *confused* with a rash (Str).... Ans: ALLERGY

(7) Tea (Anag) *is used* for this application (Str).......Ans: EAT

(8) Nigel (Anag) *used* marbles (Str)..............Ans: ELGIN

DOWN

(1) Pea can (Anag) *be made into* an appetizer (Str)............
Ans: CANAPE

(2) Rates (Anag) *make* me bring these to my eyes (Str)........
Ans: TEARS

(4) A manly (Anag) *sort* but still a novice (Str)... Ans: LAYMAN

(5) Petal (Anag) *serves up* my dinner on it (Str)....Ans: PLATE

7

WORD EXCHANGING

A standard straight crossword is nothing more than a matter of word exchanging, SMALL DRINK (3) = NIP, FATHER (3) = DAD, BIRD (4) = DOVE (or ROOK, FOWL, TERN etc). The Cryptic Crossword also uses these word exchanges, but as 'portions' of a clue answer. These are strung together to form the composite word (or words) required for the answer. Straight Crosswords are frequently one word answers, but a cryptic answer may be a whole sentence. Of course there are literally thousands of words that may be exchanged for other words, limited only by the English language. Here are a few that are used so frequently by compilers of Cryptic Crosswords that they have become commonplace:

Able	CAN	Mark	SCAR
Agent	SPY or REP	Married	WED
Allow	LET	Member	LEG or ARM
Beer	ALE	Mother	MA
Behold	LO	Noise	ROW
Communist	RED	Observe	SEE
Company	FIRM	Sailor	TAR
Dog	CUR	Speed	RATE
Employ	USE	Sum	ADD
Exam	TEST	Taxi	CAB
Father	PA	Team	SIDE
First man	ADAM	Thanks	TA
First woman	EVE	Vehicle	CAR
Girl	SHE, HER, LASS	Wager	BET
Gun	STEN or ARM	Worker	HAND, ANT or BEE
Looker	EYE	Writer	PEN
Man	HE or HIM	You and I	WE or US

Some of the words given above are reversible, Able-CAN, Can-ABLE, She-HER, Her-SHE, Arm-GUN, Gun-ARM etc.

No-one can be expected to memorize instantly the words above, but reading through them will give an understanding of the logical process of word exchanging in cryptic crosswords.

It is especially important to insert the mental commas with these clues as frequently there are several to a clue.

The word exchanges listed on the previous page are included in the more comprehensive list (which may be used for reference) starting on page 156.

Examples of word exchanging clues follow. (' / ' indicates the mental comma insertion, and again 'Str.' indicates the Straight Clue.)

THE FIRST MAN AND A WORKER WERE VERY DETERMINED. (7)
The first man (ADAM) / and a worker (ANT) / were very determined (Str.)
Answer: ADAMANT

MARK ALLOWED A SHADE OF RED. (7)
Mark (SCAR) / allowed (LET) / a shade of red (Str.)
Answer: SCARLET

YOU AND I GET OLDER BUT STILL HAVE A FUNCTION. (5)
You and I (US) / get older (AGE) / but still have a function (Str.)
Answer: USAGE

THE WOMAN AND HIM GIVE A NAME. (6)
The woman (HER) / and him (MAN) / give a name (Str.)
Answer: HERMAN

THE VEHICLE IS NOT HERE TO GET THE SEED. (7)
The vehicle (CAR) / is not here (AWAY) / to get the seed (Str.)
Answer: CARAWAY.

Obviously these clues may be used with a mixture of other types of clue.

In the next two small sample crosswords I shall use other words to be 'exchanged' as well as a selection from the above list.

8

WORD EXCHANGING CROSSWORDS

No. 1

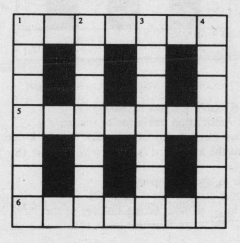

ACROSS
(1) Overtake charged particle with emotion. (7)
(5) A listener by the bird's house, that's serious. (7)
(6) A crime works with hollow bones. (7)
DOWN
(1) Father leases property for my mum and him. (7)
(2) Fight and beat the ancient military man. (7)
(3) Not outside shirts to put one's money into. (7)
(4) Take home Mr. Dawson a bar of chocolate. (7)

No. 2

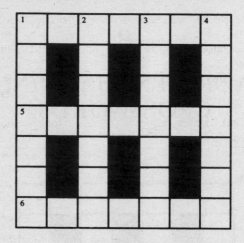

ACROSS
(1) Transport heavy weights in boxes. (7)
(5) Football Association has arms to secure. (7)
(6) Shortly on the first day of the week, the lock operators will show you the animals. (7)
DOWN
(1) Establish to cheat company. (7)
(2) Communist cover a brave man. (7)
(3) Not off to go without taking holiday in the services. (2,5)
(4) The main heirs are four this year. (7)

Answers to Word Exchanging Crosswords

No. 1

ACROSS

(1) Overtake (PASS) / charged particle (ION) / with emotion. (Str. clue).   Ans: PASSION

(5) A listener (EAR) / by the bird's house (NEST) / that's serious (Str. clue).   Ans: EARNEST

(6) A crime (SIN) / works with (USES) / hollow bones (Str. clue).
                                                                 Ans: SINUSES

DOWN

(1) Father (PA) / leases property (RENTS) / for my mum and him (Str. clue).   Ans: PARENTS

(2) Fight (SPAR) / and beat (TAN) / the ancient military man (Str. clue).   Ans: SPARTAN

(3) Not outside (IN) / shirts (VESTS) / to put one's money into (Str. clue).   Ans: INVESTS

(4) Take home (NEST) / Mr. Dawson (LES) (as in the late comedian) / a bar of chocolate (Str. clue).   Ans: NESTLES

No. 2

ACROSS

(1) Transport (CAR) / heavy weights (TONS) / in boxes (Str. clue).
                                                                 Ans: CARTONS

(5) Football Association (FA) (note: F.A. is an abbreviation, which will be covered in depth later) / has arms (STENS) / to secure (Str. clue).   Ans: FASTENS

(6) Shortly on the first day of the week (shortly 'indicates' the abbreviation) (MON) / the lock operators (KEYS) / will show you the animals (Str. clue).   Ans: MONKEYS

DOWN

(1) Establish (Str. clue) / to cheat (CON) / company (FIRM).
                                                                 Ans: CONFIRM

(2) Communist (RED) / cover (SKIN) / a brave man (Str. clue).
                                                                 Ans: REDSKIN

(3) Not off (ON) / to go without taking (LEAVE) / holiday in the services (Str. clue).   Ans: ON LEAVE

(4) The main (SEA) / heirs (SONS) / are four this year (Slightly Cryptic Straight clue).   Ans: SEASONS

9

A WORD HIDDEN IN TWO WORDS

A word hidden in two words type of clue is one that conceals the answer within a given clue sentence.

Look for the prompt from the compiler that it is this type of clue. Then read through the words provided, taking the latter part of one word, and the former part of the following word until a whole word is uncovered that complements the straight clue that is given in the clue sentence. E.g.

AMONG THE WEED I'LL FIND A HERB (4)

Reading through the sentence there is no such word as ONGT, NGTH, THEW etc. but suddenly there is a word, DILL, which happens to be a herb. But again, how is this type of clue indicated by the compiler?

As always (always! There's no such word in cryptic crosswords!) there is normally a prompt, or keyword,

e.g. among, in, inside, within, part of, coming from, from, contain / s / ed / ing, holding, out of, etc. The most common is 'in'. All these words indicate that the word sought is contained within the following or preceding text.

More examples with the keywords bracketed:

THE SUSSEX COUNTY TOWN (IN) A LITT*LE WES*TERN PART (5)

Ans: LEWES

POWDER (OBTAINED FROM) CAPI*TAL CUM*BRIA (6)   Ans: TALCUM

(INSIDE) DAV*ID EAS*ILY HAD NOTIONS (5)   Ans: IDEAS

(SOME OF) THE FORE*MAN AGED*, BUT HE STILL COPED (7)

Ans: MANAGED

GO TO (PART OF) *RICH TER*RAIN TO FIND EARTHQUAKE SCALE (7)

Ans: RICHTER

(FROM) LITT*LE PERS*ONS TO OLD SUFFERERS (6)   Ans: LEPERS

10

NUMBERS REPRESENTING LETTERS

Numbers, numeric words and Roman numerals will frequently be used to obtain a letter, or a string of letters, which then contribute to other clues of various types to solve the straight clue. Shown here are examples of the most frequently used numbers and numeric words that represent letters.

Nothing, Zero, Nil	indicates	an	O
One	"	"	I
5 or five	"	a	V
10 or ten	"	an	X
20 or twenty	"	the word	SCORE
50 or fifty	indicates	an	L
100 or one hundred	"	the letters TON or C	
500 or five hundred	"	a	D
1000 or one thousand	indicates	an	M

Here are some examples of their usage (underlined words indicate the straight clue):

NOTHING ONE TAKES TO FIFTY WILL LUBRICATE (3)
Nothing = O, one = I, takes to fifty = L, will lubricate Ans: OIL

IT TAKES FIVE HUNDRED TO ONE THOUSAND TO LOWER THE LIGHT (3)
Five hundred = D, one = I, thousand = M, to lower the light
Ans: DIM

HE IS 50-50 TO ARRIVE AT SATAN'S HOME (4)
He (HE) is 50-50 (LL) to arrive at Satan's home Ans: HELL

TWENTY OF THE MANAGEMENT KEEPS THE RUNNING TOTAL (10)
Twenty (SCORE) of the management (BOARD) keeps the running total Ans: SCOREBOARD

FIFTY-ONE AND FIVE HUNDRED GOT TO THE TOP (3)
Fifty (L) one (I) and five hundred (D) got to the top Ans: LID

11

ABBREVIATIONS

In a similar way a letter or letters can be acquired by the use of ABBREVIATIONS. There are too many abbreviated words to list in their entirety, but I give examples of some of the more frequently used.

A

About	RE	Bomb	H or A
Abstainer	TT	Bounced	RD
Account	AC	Britain	UK
Accountant	CA		
Afterthought	PS	**C**	
Against	V	Capone	AL
Agent	REP	Carbon	C
Alien	ET	Care of	CO
Amateur	A	Church	CH or CE
America	US	Clergyman	DD
American lawyer	DA	Coin	P or D
American soldier	GI	Cold	C
Apartment	APT	Company	CO
Apprentice	L	Compère	MC
Army	TA	Concerning	RE
Article	A	Copper	D, P, PC or CU
Artist	RA	Credit	CR
Attorney	DA	Current	AC or DC

B

Best	AI	**D**	
Bible	OT or NT	Day	MON, TUES, WED, etc
Bill	AC or AD	Degree	MA or BA
Bob	S	Direction	N, E, S or W
		Doctor	DR, MD, GP, MO

E

Each	EA
Editor	ED
Example	EG
Exercise	PE or PT
Extra Large	XL

F

Fahrenheit	F
Father	PA
Fifty Fifty	LL
Firm	CO
Flat	APT
Foot	FT
Football Assoc	FA
For example	EG
For instance	EG
Former	EX

G

George	G
Gold	AU
Good man	ST
Gunner/s	RA

H

Hard	H
Hesitate	ER
Holy man	ST
Home counties	SE
Hospital	H
Hot	H

I

I am	IM
In charge	IC
Iron	FE

J

Jack	J or TAR
Jolson	AL
Journalist	ED

J

Judge	JP
Junction	T

K

Kick off	KO
Kind of square	T
King	G or GR
Kiss	X
Knight	KT
Knockout	KO

L

Large	OS or L
Last month	DEC
Leader	PM
Learner	L
Left	L
Liner	QE
Loud	F

M

Magistrate	JP
Main road	AI
Manuscript	MS
Marines	RM
Medal	VC, GM, GC etc
Mediterranean	MED
Monarch	ER
Morning	AM
Mother	MA
Motorway	MI
Myself	ME

N

Navy	RN
Nazis	SS
Never never	HP
New York	NY
Nil	O

No good .... US
North East .... NE
North West .... NW
Note .... A through to G
Number .... See page 31

O

Odds .... SP
Officer ..... SM, OC, COL, etc
Old Bob .... S
Old Boy .... OB
Old flame .... EX
Old Penny .... D
Old time .... BC
On board .... SS
Operation .... OP
Orient/al .... E
Outsize .... OS

P

Parking .... P
Party ...... DO, CON, LAB, LIB
Penny .... P
Point .... N, E, S, W
Pole .... N or S
Policeman .... MP, PC, DI
Politician .... MP
Port L
Post Office .... PO
Post Script .... PS
Pound .... LB or L
Prime Minister .... PM
Pupil L

Q

Queen .... R or ER
Quiet .... P

R

Railway .... RY or BR
Record .... CD, LP or EP
Redcap .... MP

Red Cross .... RC
Regarding .... RE
Regiment .... RA etc
Regina .... R
Religion .... CE or RC
Right .... R
Ring .... O
Rolls .... RR
Royal Marines .... RM

S

Sailor .... AB
Sapper .... RE
Sauce .... HP
Ship .... SS
Shirt .... T
Short time ..... SEC, MIN, HR
Side XI
Silver .... AG
Size .... DIM
Soft .... P
Soldier ..... RE, SM, COL, etc
South East .... SE
South West .... SW
Spaniard .... EL
Starboard .... R
State ...... NY, CAL, FLA, etc
Street .... ST
Student L
Sub .... U
Sunday .... S

T

Tar .... AB
Tax .... VAT
Teetotal .... TT
Television .... TV
Territorial Army .... TA
Thanks .... TA
That is .... IE
Theologian .... DD
The French ...... LE or LA
The Spanish .... EL

Time ..... AM, PM, BC or AD		Victory V	
Tin .... SN		Vote X	
Tory .... CON			
Trains .... BR		**W**	
Turning .... U		Was .... EX	
		Way .... ST or RD	
U		Weight .... TON, LB, OZ	
Under .... SUB		Women's group .... WI	
Unit .... ONE			
United States .... US		**Y**	
		Year .... AGE or YR	
V			
Versus .... VIE or V		**Z**	
Very quiet .... PP		Zero .... O	

Examples of Abbreviation Clues

Straight Clues indicated by (Str.)

DOCTOR AND A MOTHER MADE A PLAY (5)
Doctor (DR) and a (A) mother (MA) made a play (Str.).

Ans: DRAMA

THE PRIME MINISTER WENT ROUND THE QUEEN FOR A HAIRDO (4)
The Prime Minister (PM) went round (*went round* indicates to wrap the letters around the next letters arrived at from the given clue, more on this later) the Queen (ER) for a hairdo (Str.).   Ans: PERM

FOUR POINTS CONFUSED UP TO DATE INFORMATION (4)
Four points (N, E, S, W) confused (indicates an Anagram of N E S W) up to date information (Str.).   Ans: NEWS

AN AGENT OF THE BEST COMMUNIST WILL GET IT FIXED (8)
An agent (REP) of the best (AI) communist (RED) will get it fixed (Str.).   Ans: REPAIRED

TAKE A NOTE THIS MORNING TO MOTHER, IT'S A GREEK LETTER (5)
Take a note (G) this morning (AM) to mother (MA) it's a Greek letter (Str.).   Ans: GAMMA

FOR GETTING A DEGREE TWO STUDENTS HAD A BIG PARTY (4)
For getting a degree (BA) two students (LL) had a big party (Str.).
Ans: BALL

BOAST REGARDING RAILWAY SILVER (4)
Boast (Str.) railway (BR) silver (AG).   Ans: BRAG

12

DOUBLE MEANING WORDS

I said on page 17 that there is almost always a Straight clue within the given Clue sentence, which is either the opening or the closing word/s. With the Double Meaning clue the whole clue is straight. So what, you may ask, makes it a Cryptic clue? The answer is that it is a Straight clue, but only when it is read in the correct context. I will explain.

Perhaps the most misleading aspect of Cryptic Crosswords is the insertion of words that have more than one meaning or Double Meaning words. These clues are the very essence of, and are largely responsible for, making the Cryptic crossword as we know it, Cryptic.

There are many words in the complicated English language that are spelt the same, but have entirely different meanings, e.g. FAIR (blonde or unbiased), CUT (sever or portion), LIGHT (not heavy or bright), FAT (obese or lard), BULB (plant or electric light), REST (relax or balance of), IRON (to press or metal), etc. These words are sadistically used by the compiler deliberately to deceive or mislead you into reading the clue in the wrong context, even to the extent of using words that are technically bad English (again, to be demonstrated later). You must develop an awareness of this and understand that when a clue appears to be relatively straight, be certain that it is not! In fact, a good indication that the Double Meaning clue is in use is that the clue will appear to be suspiciously straight.

These are probably the most common causes of the unsolved clue, and it's very frustrating to read the answer the next day and realize that what seemed an impossible clue, when read in another context, is really quite simple. Here are some examples:
(the double meaning words are underlined):

THIS FLOWER IS THE BIGGEST IN AFRICA (4)
Before you consult every horticultural book in the British Museum, the clue does not mean a plant. It is asking for the biggest FLOW-ER, as in a river. (This is an example of the bad use of English I referred to earlier.) The answer then, of course, is NILE.

REQUESTED TO COME TO A PARTY (10)
Now that's simple and straightforward enough, "INVITATION". No, it's not that simple. This is a Cryptic crossword clue, so what other

type of party is there? The party in this case, is a political party. Now it's easy. CAMPAIGNED.

THIS BOX IS FREE OF CHARGE (4,7)
Because the word "FREE" is used, you immediately associate the word CHARGE with a fee, but in this instance it actually means voltage, as in a battery. So then the answer is obvious, FLAT BATTERY.

A DEFINITE BENEFIT IN COURT (9)
The COURT in the clue is not a Law Court but in fact a tennis court. So the answer is ADVANTAGE.

ONLY TO BE WORN INSIDE (7,4)
INSIDE doesn't just mean indoors, it is slang for prison, and a CONVICT SUIT is what is worn inside.

GET DOWN FROM HERE (7)
You immediately associate getting down with descending, but were this the case the possible answers would be many and there is no other indication of where it should be from. Down is also a part of a bird's plumage. So the answer is PLUMAGE.

THIS WILL TELL THE TIME (8,5)
Again, you will think of the obvious, but were it a simple timepiece then the clue would be straight, not Cryptic, and there is no indication of what type of timepiece is required. The answer required is the only timepiece that can literally "tell" the time, which of course is a SPEAKING CLOCK.

PLACE TO LEARN TO DRIVE (4,6)
I am quite confident that you understand the double meaning word clue now, so you will have no trouble in realising that the word 'DRIVE' does not refer to the obvious, which is driving a car, but driving as a golfer would. So the answer of course is GOLF COURSE.

THE COST OF BEING LATE (7,8)
Apart from being overdue, it also means deceased, so the answer is FUNERAL EXPENSES.

RESULT OF A SUSPENDED SENTENCE (5,7)
This does not mean what we know of as encouragement not to commit another crime, quite the reverse. The clue is straighter than you may think. It means literally suspended or hanged.
The answer sought is DEATH PENALTY.
(Imagine the reaction of a keen Cryptic Crossworder appearing in court and being given a suspended sentence!)

Now, using a mixture of the different types of clues that we have learned so far, try and complete your first full Cryptic Crossword.

13

FULL SAMPLE CROSSWORD

ACROSS

(1) Used to divide ground when swordfighting. (7)
(7) A plea not to die from Popeye's girl. (5)
(8) Baby and little Alan altogether. (5)
(9) Yell red perhaps for the OAP's. (7)
(12) Mixed tech drawing. (4)
(14) Sea tern changes direction. (7)
(17) Following Doctor's call. (4)

(18) It's light to carry. (7)
(22) Was once on the stage to be precise. (5)
(23) Lift part of Toni Curtis. (5)
(24) Will too much sun make him short tempered? (7)

DOWN
(1) Parent priest. (6)
(2) Spot Bill. (6)
(3) This lea contains emerald place. (4)
(4) Olympic winner. (4)
(5) Support in Southend. (4)
(6) Denny, take a point and refuse privilege. (4)
(10) Not sooner be successive. (5)
(11) Make money out of Dave Arnold. (4)
(13) Soldier's stop. (4)
(15) Cancel the North East door. (6)
(16) Declared Ted sat around. (6)
(18) Fifty dined but were overdue. (4)
(19) Two lots of refuse. (2,2)
(20) Fruit that's less soft, but one apiece. (4)
(21) Amphibian went out. (4)

Answers to Full Sample Crossword
ACROSS
(1)   Double Straight clue: Used to divide ground / when sword-fighting.   Ans: FENCING
(7)   Cryptic first part: A plea not to die (O'LIVE). Straight clue: Popeye's girl (Olive Oyl).   Ans: OLIVE
(8)   Word Exchange first part: Baby (TOT). Abbreviation of Little Alan (AL). Straight clue: altogether.   Ans: TOTAL
(9)   Anagram of Yell red (indicated by the word 'perhaps'). Straight clue: the OAP's.   Ans: ELDERLY
(12)   Anagram of tech (indicated by the word 'mixed'). Straight clue: drawing.   Ans: ETCH
(14)   Anagram of Sea tern (indicated by the word 'changes'). Straight clue: direction.   Ans: EASTERN
(17)   Straight first part: Following. Cryptic second part: Doctor's call (as he leans out of the door of his examination room).
                                                                  Ans: NEXT
(18)   Double Meaning clue: It's light, means illumination not weight; a light you carry that will fit the answer grid.
                                                               Ans: LANTERN
(22)   Word Exchange: Was once (EX). Cryptic second part: on the stage (ACT as in 'an' act, not 'to' act). Straight clue: to be precise.   Ans: EXACT
(23)   Straight clue first: Lift. 'Part of' indicates a Word From Two Words clue: TONI CUrtis. (The fact that it is not the correct spelling of the actor's name is not relevant.)   Ans: TONIC
(24)   Single Cryptic clue. (Remember that the question mark indicates a clue a little more cryptic than usual.)
                                                               Ans: HOTHEAD

DOWN
(1)   Double Straight clue: Parent / Priest.   Ans: FATHER
(2)   Double Straight clue: Spot / Bill. (If you spot something you notice it; a bill, as in billboard, is a notice).   Ans: NOTICE
(3)   A Word From Two Words type of clue: ThIS LEa contains (the word 'contains' indicates this). Straight clue: Emerald place.
                                                                  Ans: ISLE
(4)   Double Meaning clue: It is worded to lead you to believe a 'person' is required for the answer, by using the word winner instead of 'prize'.   Ans: GOLD
(5)   Straight clue first: Support (a PIER is a support). Cryptic clue: in Southend.   Ans: PIER

(6)   Cryptic clue first: Denny, take a point (take away a point i.e. North or N to leave DENY). Straight clue: refuse privilege.

Ans: DENY

(10) Double Straight clue: Not sooner / be successive is to follow or come LATER.   Ans: LATER

(11) Straight clue: make money. Word From Two Words clue, indicated by the words 'out of': DavE ARNold.   Ans: EARN

(13) Single Cryptic clue (almost straight): Soldier's stop.

Ans: HALT

(15) Straight clue: Cancel. Abbreviation clue second: North (N) East (E). Door, Word Exchange clue (another word meaning door could be gate).   Ans: NEGATE

(16) Straight clue: Declared. Anagram: Ted sat around (the word 'around' indicates the anagram).   Ans: STATED

(18) Numbers Representing Letters clue: Fifty (L). Word Exchange clue: dined (ATE). Straight clue: overdue.   Ans: LATE

(19) Double Meaning clue: refuse means a denial, not rubbish.

Ans: NO NO

(20) Cryptic clue: Fruit that's less soft (less means take away the abbreviation of soft, which is P), (P)each. Straight clue: one apiece.   Ans: EACH

(21) Straight clue: Lizard. Anagram of went (the word 'out' indicates the anagram).   Ans: NEWT

14

REVISION I

If you found any of the clues too difficult to answer, I'm sure you understood once it was explained.

I now need to re-emphasise the importance of two particular points I made earlier.

The Mental Comma

You must mentally insert those commas to break down the clue sentence. If you read a clue correctly, when read aloud it should sound as though you were having great trouble in reading at all. This is to say that each word, or small group of words, should sound staggered as a result of the mental insertion of commas. The purpose of this is that, as you become familiar with certain words, you can actually obtain the answer before getting to the straight clue (providing the straight clue is at the end of the sentence and providing there is a straight clue). To demonstrate this I will give a few simple clues and enter in brackets the words, or letters, that should eventually become obvious to replace the ones given in the clue. I say 'obvious' in the way that one fluent in reading a foreign language does not have to convert a particular word that is read into English in order to understand its meaning.

(A '/' denotes the mental comma.)

FATHER IS NOT OUT WHAT AN ACHE (4)
Father (PA) / is not out (IN) / what an ache (Straight clue).

Ans: PAIN

THE BUSINESS IN THIS PLACE WILL REMAIN UNITED (6)
The Business (CO, short for COmpany) / in this place (HERE) / will remain united (Straight clue). Ans: COHERE

THE GOOD MAN CAN FIND A HOME FOR THE HORSE (6)
The good man (ST) / can (ABLE) / find a home for the horse (Straight clue). Ans: STABLE

One of the wonderful peculiarities of the cryptic crossword is that you can, once the ability to recognize certain clues has been established, actually obtain answers of which you had never previously heard.

E.g. COMMUNIST THE FOURTH 4th TO YOU AND I WILL BE REINSTATED. (9)

Communist (RED) / the fourth (IV) / 4th (IV) / to you and I (US) / will be reinstated. Ans: REDIVIVUS

Now it is possible that you are familiar with this word, but I was not. Yet I would easily have obtained the answer from the clues given. The word actually means restored.

15

REVISION II

The Open Mind
Double meaning words

One of the qualities possessed by the Cryptic Crossworder that sets him aside from normal *homo sapiens*, is the ability to read words or sentences with an entirely open mind. This enables him to spot the many, many Double Meaning words used by the compiler to deliberately confuse, or lay a false trail.

E.g. HE'S A BRAVE MAN (6)

You immediately think (as the compiler wants you to) of a heroic type, but then that would be a straight clue. So what other meaning could the word Brave have? Ans: INDIAN

INMATE'S TIME FOR BREAKFAST (8)

Because the word 'breakfast' is used, you interpret the word 'time' with an O'clock association, but after inserting the mental comma the word now becomes time in a different sense, and we have a Double Straight clue.

Inmate's time / for breakfast. Ans: PORRIDGE

LENGTH OF RULER (5)

You've worked this out already haven't you? We are not talking about a measuring device, but a monarch. Ans: REIGN

CHOKE WILL GIVE CARBURETTOR MORE FUEL (8)
This seems a strange clue. It appears to be a statement not a question requiring an answer. The word 'CHOKE' has a double meaning. Because the balance of the clue concerns a motor of some description, we have tunnel vision believing the choke is what we use on a cold morning. But it also means to strangle. Ans: THROTTLE

This open-mindedness is probably the most difficult aspect of solving cryptic clues, but once mastered, you are THERE!!!!

> **(1) Insert the mental commas**
>
> **(2) Keep an open mind**

16

VARIOUS OTHER TYPES OF CLUES

Sounds Like (Homophones)

Clues often incorporate a 'Sounds Like' element and will generally form the cryptic section of the sentence. The best way to explain this type of clue is with examples:

THIS ONE-EYED SEA LORD SOUNDS LIKE NELLIE'S BOY (6)
This one-eyed Sea Lord (Straight clue), sounds like (indicates the homophone), Nellie's boy (Nel's son). **Ans:** NELSON

VENISON SUPPLIER SOUNDS EXPENSIVE (4)
Venison supplier (Straight clue), sounds (indicator), expensive (dear). **Ans:** DEER

TO BE HONEST I HEAR IT'S FRENCH CURRENCY (5)
To be honest (Straight clue), I hear (indicator), it's French currency (Franc). **Ans:** FRANK

There are few words that indicate this type of clue, SOUNDS LIKE and WE HEAR being the most common, but SAYS, SPOKEN, IT'S SAID and HEARD or IT'S HEARD will also be used.

Leader and Head

This is a very straightforward type of clue. It has nothing to do with a leader as in boss or Commander. What it actually means is, take the first letter of the preceding word and use it to contribute to the make up of the answer. E.g.

TRAIL LEADER REQUEST FOR ASSIGNMENT (4)

Trail leader (T), request (ASK), for assignment (Straight clue).

Ans: TASK

A similar type of clue to obtain the first letter, is HEAD. When HEAD is used it means take the first letter of the actual word that HEAD is the latter part of. E.g.

THE MOTORHEAD TOOK FOOD TO A FRIEND (4)

Motorhead (M), took food (ATE), to a friend (Straight clue).

Ans: MATE

Endless, Headless

The reverse of the previous type of clue. This is used to remove a letter from a given word, the remainder being used in, or for, the answer. E.g.

BOY'S NAME FROM ENDLESS TIME (3)

Tim / e   Ans: TIM

(This may also be indicated by TAIL OFF or TAIL AWAY.)

HEADLESS MASCOT ARRIVED AT RACECOURSE (5)

Headless (indicator), m/ascot, arrived at racecourse.   Ans: ASCOT

Another variation of this type of clue that indicates the removal of a letter or letters may be MIDDLE OR CENTRE REMOVED. E.g.

REMOVE CENTRE OF TIMBERS TO MAKE CLOCKS (6)

Remove centre (indicator to remove middle letter), of tim B ers to make clocks (Straight clue).   Ans: TIMERS

Initially

To obtain more than one 'first letter', the word INITIALLY is used. This means precisely that. Take the first letter from the string of words preceding or succeeding the word INITIALLY. E.g. INITIALLY TRANSPORT AND BUSES LEAGUE EMPLOYERS MAY SIT ROUND THIS (5)

Initially (indicating word), Transport And Buses League Employers (T-A-B-L-E), may sit round this (Straight clue).   Ans: TABLE

SOUTHERN COMPANY AND RESERVES INITIALLY MADE A MARK (4)
Southern Company And Reserves, initially (indicator), made a mark
(Straight clue).   Ans: SCAR

Inside

If the compiler wishes a letter or a string of letters to be inserted into
letters that we already have, then this can be indicated by several
words.
INSIDE, WITHIN, BETWEEN, CONTAINED IN, INSERT, INTO, SWALLOWED
BY, etc. E.g.
ONE CAN GO INSIDE PLACE TO GET FISH (6)
One (I), can go inside place (PLA-I-CE), to get fish   Ans: PLAICE

FIFTY ENTERED PARTY, A PROPORTION (6)
Fifty (L), entered party (PART-L-Y), a proportion   Ans: PARTLY

Reversed

The word REVERSED or any other word that indicates such e.g.
BACKING, COMING BACK, RETURNING, TURNING ROUND etc., means
exactly that. The compiler requires the word given to be reversed to
obtain another word or string of letters. E.g.
WARD RETURNED THE RAFFLE (4)
Ward returned (DRAW), the raffle.   Ans: DRAW
REVERSE PART THAT CATCHES (4)
Reverse part (TRAP), that catches.   Ans: TRAP

Rising

The word RISING is used in a situation where the word given is
required to be reversed as before, but in this instance, only with
'Down' clues.
Other words that may indicate this are, COMING UP,
GOING UP, GETTING UP, UP, LIFTED etc. E.g.

TRAP ED GETTING UP TO LEAVE (6)
When trap ed is written 'upwards' the result is DEPART.

STAR LAID UP OLD TIMEPIECE (7)
This clue requires a word exchange first, followed by a 'whole' word.
Star (SUN), up (indicator), laid (DIAL), old timepiece (Straight
clue).   Ans: SUNDIAL

LIFT NET AFTER NINE. (3)
Lift (indicator), net (TEN), after nine (Straight clue).   Ans: TEN

Poetry

A little out of character maybe, as they seem to be straight clues, lines of poetry, Biblical, famous quotes or speeches may be used with a missing word. The word, once it is found, is the whole answer. E.g.

LET EVERY SOUL BE - - - - - - - UNTO THE HIGHER POWERS (7)
(Romans Chapter 13)   Ans: SUBJECT

Whole Words

'Unmolested' whole words or single letters are also used to contribute to an answer but I'm afraid nothing will indicate this. E.g.

ONE HUNDRED AND ONE APPOINTMENTS FOR THE MEN STANDING FOR ELECTION (10)
One hundred (C), and (Whole word AND), one (I), appointments (DATES), for the men standing for election (Straight clue).
                                              Ans: CANDIDATES

GOOD MAN OR MY CONNECTION GIVES BAD AFFAIR (6,12)
Good man (ST), or my (Whole words ORMY), connection (RELATIONSHIP), give bad affair (Straight clue).
                                    Ans: STORMY RELATIONSHIP

WAGER ON A GREEK LETTER (4)
Wager (BET), on a (Whole word A), Greek letter (Straight clue).
                                                     Ans: BETA

First / Before

When these words are used they indicate that the clue given must be placed before the latter clue. E.g.

FIRE COMPANY'S FIRST RUSSIAN HORSEMAN (7)
Fire (SACK), company's (COS), first (Indicator), Russian horseman (Straight clue).   Ans: COSSACK

BEING REFLECTIVE WAS FIRST VERY COSTLY (9)
Being reflective (PENSIVE), was (EX), first (Indicator), very costly (Straight clue).   Ans: EXPENSIVE

AN EXAMPLE OF A POSE NOT OUT BEFORE (8)
An example (Straight clue) of a pose (STANCE), not out (IN), before (Indicator).   Ans: INSTANCE

The Single Cryptic

Single Cryptic clues are very common. One must look upon this type of clue as a variation of the Double Meaning clue, but as purer Cryptic. Indeed, it stretches the limits of 'fairness' as it frequently

breaks the rules of pure English. It can take the form of a statement
that *could* be seen this way, e.g.

SPANNER (5,6)   Ans: FORTH BRIDGE
(a bridge 'spans' a gap)
NIPPER (4)   Ans: CRAB
MATE (3,2,4)   Ans: END OF GAME
....or as a question, almost a request to allow it (explained below).

The Single Cryptic with Question Mark
Apart from the normal application of a question mark, used with the
Single Cryptic clue it also indicates a more tongue in cheek answer.
This type of clue truly requires the 'open mind'. E.g.

TOP DRAWER? (3,4)   Ans: VAN GOGH
A NIGHTSPOT? (4)   Ans: STAR
CANINE TABLE LAYER? (6)   Ans: SETTER

Either Way
BOTH WAYS, WHICHEVER WAY. One of the rare straightforward clues,
this means that the compiler is looking for a palindrome (a word that
reads the same backwards as forwards), e.g.

EITHER WAY SHE'S A LADY (5)   Ans: MADAM

WHICHEVER WAY YOU LOOK AT IT, IT'S STILL A BOAT (5)
                                                         Ans: KAYAK

Continuation Line ....
A clue which is succeeded by a continuation line of dots, signifies
that the following clue somehow pertains or relates to it. The
relationship may be a word contained within the clue, or the answer.
The reverse, of course, is true if *pre*-ceded. E.g.

(1) Relatively legal........(2-3)   Ans: IN-LAW
(4) ....or them perhaps. (6)   Ans: MOTHER (Anag)
(7) A perfect County for retiring people........(4)
                                                         Ans: BEDS
(9) ....sleeping soundly. (7)   Ans: SNORING

17

HERE ENDETH THE LESSON

Well, as far as explanations of the different kinds of clue are concerned, that's it. From here on, it's learn by example, which, from my own experience, is by far the best instruction. I hope you have understood this demonstration of clues and their solutions.

Although some may have seemed difficult, do not forget that after the first clue, you are assisted by the letters which you have already inserted!

Now let's get on with what the book is all about, solving crosswords. The answers given for the crosswords in the rest of the book will have a degree of explanatory notes, not quite as 'in depth' as the earlier ones, but nevertheless certainly more useful to beginners than the typical 'one word' (or whatever) answers that are usually given.

The Crosswords that follow are arranged at two levels;

I: Basic Cryptic Crosswords.
      Tabloid Newspaper standard (these start on page 52.)

II: More Advanced Cryptic Crosswords.
      Broadsheet Newspaper Standard therefore somewhat more difficult (these start on page 108).

As we make our way through the crosswords they will get progressively harder, but, if your understanding of "crypticism" is improving, then this will hopefully go unnoticed!

GOOD LUCK !!

PART TWO
CROSSWORDS

18

LEVEL I
BASIC CRYPTIC
CROSSWORDS

No. 1

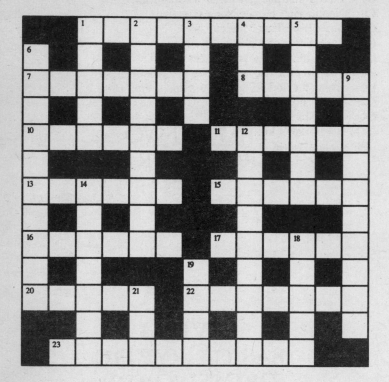

ACROSS

(1)   I hear the writing equipment just won't move. (10)
(7)   Sports ground at mid US perhaps. (7)
(8)   Car factory that should be buried. (5)
(10) Majorcan resort in a real North mess. (6)
(11) The barman's glasses are on the shelf. (6)
(13) He's always first out. (4,2)
(15) The auburn is real hot and spicy. (6)
(16) Goes by rail and works out. (6)
(17) Alley in Martin Pankhurst's part. (3,3)
(20) It's in the back or middle of the book. (5)
(22) Good man, mad peele always at church. (7)
(23) Place for growing flowers in the kids' room. (3,7)

DOWN

(1)   Find a suit and get a flat in South East. (5)
(2)   Naomi ain't moving for excitement. (9)
(3)   She's from Fair Maiden. (4)
(4)   Take a rest and play cards. (3)
(5)   Town ideal for a bookworm? (7)
(6)   Their leader had a big part in the water. (10)
(9)   Exam for athlete, go for a spin in this. (10)
(12)   It's an honour to give special licence. (9)
(14)   His naps turned out to be Continentals. (7)
(18)   It's Barker's kid. (5)
(19)   United States Queen for employer. (4)
(21)   Leon is less 50 what an age. (3)

Answers to Crossword No. 1
ACROSS
(1) STATIONARY (A Sounds Like clue: stationery, which is writing equipment, sounds like something that is static.)
(7) STADIUM (Straight clue first; an Anagram of AT MID US, indicated by the word 'perhaps'.)
(8) PLANT (Straight and Cryptic clue.)
(10) ARENAL (Straight clue: Majorcan resort; Anagram of A REAL and N which is an abbreviation of North, indicated by the word 'mess'.) An interesting point here is that the word resort could also have been used as an Anagram Indicator.
(11) OPTICS (Double Meaning clue: a pair of glasses are optics, and the containers that hold spirits are optics.)
(13) LAST IN (Single Cryptic, as in 'Last in first out'.)
(15) GINGER (Double Straight.)
(16) TRAINS (Double Straight.)
(17) TIN PAN (Word From Two Words, indicated by the word 'part'.)
     This is a name associated with areas occupied by musicians in both New York and London.
(20) SPINE (Double Straight.)
(22) STEEPLE (Abbreviation: good man = ST; an Anagram of PEELE, indicated by the word 'mad'; Straight clue: always at church.)
(23) THE NURSERY (Double Straight clue.)

DOWN
(1) SPADE (Straight clue: find a suit, as in a diamond or a spade, which is a double meaning word intended to make you think of a suit of clothing; flat = PAD; put inside, indicated by 'in'; Abbreviated South East (SE).)
(2) ANIMATION (Anagram: indicated by 'moving'; Straight clue: Excitement.)
(3) IRMA (Word From Two Words clue, indicated by the word 'from'.)
(4) NAP (Double Straight. NAP is a card game correctly called Napoleon, but commonly called Nap.)
(5) READING (Single Cryptic: should be seen as REEDING not REDDING.)
(6) ISRAELITES (Single Cryptic: Moses, their leader, parted the water.)

(9) TESTRUNNER (Exam = TEST; athlete = RUNNER; Straight clue: go for a spin in this.)

(12) PRIVILEGE (Double Straight.)

(14) SPANISH (Anagram of HIS NAPS, indicated by 'turned out'; Straight clue: Continentals.)

(18) PUPPY (Single Cryptic.)

(19) USER (Abbreviation clue: United States = US, Queen = ER; Straight clue: employer.)

(21) EON (Abbreviation: Leon less 50 (remove an L); Straight clue: what an age.)

No. 2

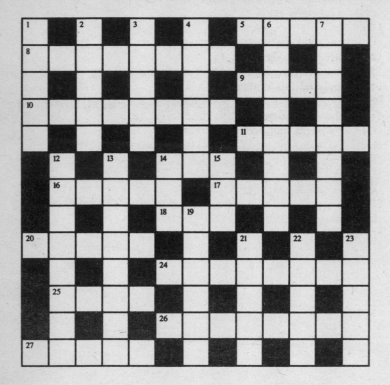

ACROSS

(5)   Stretch your neck to see the bird. (5)
(8)   Make certain after an appeal it's enjoyable. (8)
(9)   It's odds on the morning will bring meat. (4)
(10) Akin to a monster? Well similar. (8)
(11) Used to measure duration of prison sentence, right. (5)
(14) Initially British Overseas Airways will crush opposition. (3)
(16) Time before (around Anno Domini) I miss it. (5)
(17) - - - - - de la - - - - -, simply the best. (5)
(18) It will be here at any time, it's owed to me. (3)
(20) Homes for Queens or the workers. (5)
(24) Small amount to earn for making fasteners? (3,5)
(25) One factory section. (4)

(26) Young lad had enough to eat we hear. (8)

(27) Passes the cards and makes agreements. (5)

DOWN

(1) It would be a sin to share it with Eve. (5)

(2) Fifty seek mixed veg. (5)

(3) Sean, nothing moved. Do it together. (2,3)

(4) Hey! and this is magic. (6)

(6) About being put into twosomes, that's fixed. (8)

(7) When your days are, it's time to go. (8)

(12) Treatment required when corn grows too long. (8)

(13) The way to leave someone. (4,4)

(14) Where lying people go. (3)

(15) A card from a church. (3)

(19) 3 would be in this. (6)

(21) Common name for an iron worker? (5)

(22) Extinguish candle to assist breathing. (5)

(23) Recurring period to travel. (5)

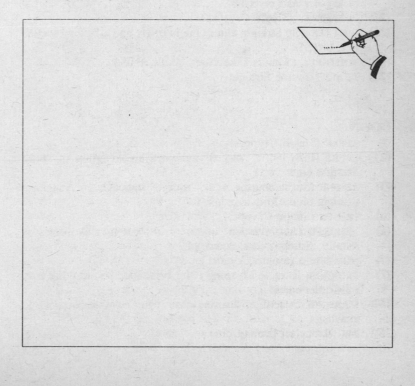

Answers to Crossword No. 2
ACROSS
(5)   CRANE (Double Straight.)

(8)   PLEASURE (Make certain = SURE, which is put after an appeal = PLEA; Straight clue: it's enjoyable.)

(9)   SPAM (Abbreviation of odds = SP, and morning = AM; Straight clue: meat.)

(10) LIKENESS (Akin to = LIKE; a monster = NESS; Straight clue: similar.)

(11) TIMER (Straight clue: used to measure; Prison sentence = TIME; right = R.)

(14) BOA (Initial clue: British Overseas Airways; will crush opposition, as a BOA constrictor would.)

(16) EVADE (Time before = EVE; 'around' means wrap eve around the next clue; Anno Domini = AD.)

(17) CREME (Quotes clue.)

(18) DUE (Double Straight.)

(20) HIVES (Double Meaning clue: it was intended that you thought of Royalty and serfs.)

(24) PIN MONEY (Single Cryptic.)

(25) UNIT (Double Straight clue: One is UNIT, and a factory section is a UNIT.)

(26) YOUTHFUL (Sounds Like clue: Youth, Full.)

(27) DEALS (Double Straight.)

DOWN
(1)   APPLE (Single Cryptic.)

(2)   LEEKS (Fifty = L; 'mixed' indicates an Anagram of SEEK; Straight clue: veg.)

(3)   AS ONE (Sean; nothing = O, 'moved' indicates an Anagram; Straight clue: do it together.)

(4)   PRESTO (Single Cryptic.)

(6)   REPAIRED (Abbreviation: about = RE; put into twosomes = PAIRED; Straight clue: fixed.)

(7)   NUMBERED (Single Cryptic.)

(12) PEDICURE (Double Meaning clue: I intended you to think corn meant the cereal.)

(13) MAKE WILL (Double Meaning clue: you 'leave' to someone in a will.)

(14) BED (Double Meaning clue.)

(15) ACE (Straight clue: A card; Whole Word: A; church = CE.)

(19) UNISON (Single Cryptic. When an actual number is given, it can often mean, as it does in this case, the number of a clue elsewhere in the crossword. Clue No. 3 is AS ONE.)
(21) SMITH (Double Straight clue.)
(22) SNUFF (Double Straight clue. Snuff is inhaled to clear nasal passages.)
(23) CYCLE (Double Straight clue.)

No. 3

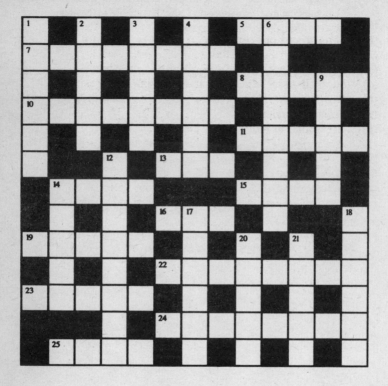

ACROSS
- (5) Give assistance to man on board. (4)
- (7) He needs a lot of room to work in. (8)
- (8) A callus fruit? (5)
- (10) Saved for a rainy day? (8)
- (11) Nowadays a small party will improvise..... (2,3)
- (13) ......and yet another time nothing made much about nothing. (3)
- (14) Instruction on pitch for a player. (4)
- (15) Reduce bonus and make responsible. (4)
- (16) Came out East to move off centre.......... (3)
- (19) ....or round the middle. (5)
- (22) Tailless Moss Viper is bad, but gets better. (8)
- (23) Weight of a gem? (5)

(24) A vessel to lodge in the cabinet. (8)
(25) Lobby the house of lords. (4)

DOWN

(1) Shrewd sort of statue. (6)
(2) He got Joan in the Club. (5)
(3) Possibly Buzz Aldrin was given this clue number. (5)
(4) Football Association lied about having lost. (6)
(6) Had a crash? Then account to C.I.D. about ten. (8)
(9) Training guides? (5)
(12) Al's prone to move in private. (8)
(14) Pop record? (5)
(17) Weapon contributes to our protection. (6)
(18) Within prison. (6)
(20) Brave group from Mount Ribense. (5)
(21) Used to give a good tanning. (1,1,3)

Answers to Crossword No. 3
ACROSS
(5) HAND (Double Straight clue. To give assistance is to give a hand; man on board could be a deck hand.)

(7) SPACEMAN (Single Cryptic.)

(8) ACORN (Whole word: A; Callus = CORN; an acorn is the fruit of the Oak tree.)

(10) UMBRELLA (It's fifty-fifty whether you related 'saving' to finances or storing. I hope it was finances or else the clue is too straight!)

(11) AD LIB (Nowadays = AD; a small party = LIB, 'small' indicating an Abbreviation, not the actual membership of the party; Straight clue: improvise.)

(13) ADO (The continuation dots indicate that this clue is relative to the last, the relativity being AD. This with nothing = O completes the clue answer.)

(14) CLEF (A 'double' Double Meaning clue: 'a player' is Cryptic for musician, and 'pitch' is to do with sound, not playing area.)

(15) ONUS (Reduce = remove a letter; Straight clue: responsible.)

(16) CAM (Out East = Remove E; a cam is an ovaloid shape.)

(19) WAIST (Relative with the words centre and middle.)

(22) IMPROVES (Tailless moss = MOS; Anagram of VIPER and MOS, indicated by 'is bad'.)

(23) STONE (Single Cryptic.)

(24) CUPBOARD (A vessel = CUP; to lodge = BOARD; Straight clue: cabinet.)

(25) HALL (Double Straight: a lobby is a hall and a Lord may live in a Hall.)

DOWN
(1) ASTUTE (Anagram of STATUE, indicated by 'sort'.)

(2) DARBY (As in Darby & Joan Club.)

(3) SEVEN (Very Cryptic: 7 Across was a SPACEMAN, as was Buzz Aldrin.)

(4) FAILED (Initials: FA; Anagram of LIED, indicated by 'about'; Straight clue: lost.)

(6) ACCIDENT (Account = AC; Whole Word, or in this case initials: CID; Anagram of TEN.)

(9) RAILS (Double Meaning Word, training, used to mislead.)

(12) PERSONAL (Anagram of AL'S PRONE, indicated by 'to move'.)

(14) CHART (Double Meaning clue: the record is not a disc, it's an account.)

(17) ARMOUR (Weapon = ARM; Whole Word: 'OUR'; Straight clue: protection.)

(18) INSIDE (Double Straight.)

(20) TRIBE (Word From Two Words, indicated by the word 'from'.)

(21) U V RAY (Double Meaning clue.)

From here on the explanations of various clues will only be given where I believe necessary.

No. 4

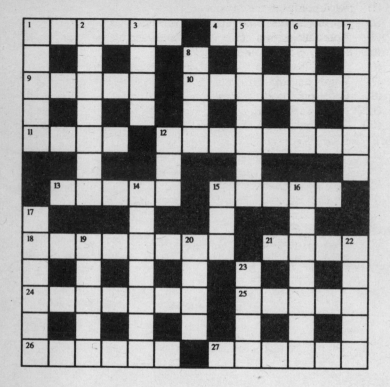

ACROSS

(1)   Sappers may pretend to relax. (6)
(4)   A stoic remake of corner moulding. (6)
(9)   Flying bomb turned agent into a snake. (5)
(10)   A floater for the card game. (7)
(11)   Bloom that needs plenty of water. (4)
(12)   One trail that leads to the East. (8)
(13)   The first best man is a builder. (5)
(15)   Way to hit, or give a belt. (5)
(18)   Bringing gifts from overseas can be taxing. (8)
(21)   Large toe nail? (4)
(24)   Orator needed to broadcast speech. (7)
(25)   Follow the road. (5)
(26)   Talk a lot about a rat net. (6)
(27)   Level description of a charmer. (6)

DOWN

(1) Avril confused the opponent. (5)

(2) Up, up in the polar region is well liked. (7)

(3) Aphrodite's child came up to be tender. (4)

(5) Happy to cheat on shelter. (7)

(6) Two fifths of the tribe are away hunting for fish. (5)

(7) Wildly ran old Mr. Palmer. (6)

(8) Boot spike to get a move on. (4)

(12) Remove tree from soaking wood. (3)

(14) One hundred the French put on the torture table to make a noise. (7)

(15) She can litigate. (3)

(16) Advocate replacing alien for nothing, will bear fruit. (7)

(17) Lighthouse inventor? (6)

(19) An endless agreement to pay for someone. (5)

(20) Mess around with a bird. (4)

(22) Obscene amount of dirt. (5)

(23) Mets returned part of the plant. (4)

Answers to Crossword No. 4
ACROSS
(1)   REPOSE (Sappers = RE (Royal Engineers); pretend = POSE; Straight clue: relax.)

(4)   SCOTIA (Anagram, indicated by 'remake'. Scotia is a 90° corner moulding.)

(9)   VIPER (Flying Bomb = VI; Agent = REP; turned = PER.)

(10) PONTOON (Technically a Double Straight although the floater is a little obscure.)

(11) LILY (Single Cryptic.)

(12) ORIENTAL (Anagram, indicated by 'that leads'.)

(13) BRICK (First best, which means the first letter of Best = B; man = RICK. Although poor English, a brick is a builder.)

(15) STRAP (Way = ST; hit = RAP; Straight clue: a belt.)

(18) DUTIABLE (Single Cryptic.)

(21) HOOF (Single Cryptic.)

(24) SPEAKER (An orator is a SPEAKER and to broadcast one needs an amplifier and speaker.)

(25) TRAIL (Double Straight.)

(26) NATTER (Anagram of RAT NET, indicated by 'about'.)

(27) SMOOTH (Double Straight.)

DOWN
(1)   RIVAL (Anagram of AVRIL indicated by 'confused'.)

(2)   POPULAR (Up meaning to reverse the word 'up', in the whole word POLAR.)

(3)   SORE (Another Rising clue but this time the whole word is used. Eros was the child of Aphrodite.)

(5)   CONTENT (Straight clue: Happy; Cheat = CON; Shelter = TENT.)

(6)   TROUT (Two fifths of the tribe = TR; are away = OUT.)

(7)   ARNOLD (Anagram of RAN OLD; Straight clue: Mr. Palmer, as in ARNOLD Palmer the famous golfer.)

(8)   SPUR (Double Straight: a boot spike is a SPUR, and to push someone on is to spur.)

(12) OAK (Remove means literally that, remove a tree from the word soaking.)

(14) CRACKLE (Hundred = C; the French = LE; 'put on' means put LE on the end of the following word, RACK which is a torture table.)

(15) SUE (Single Cryptic.)

(16) AVOCADO (Replace alien = ET, for nothing = O; the word

replace is used in a second sense, meaning to replace the letters, which indicates an Anagram of course.)

(17) EDISON (Double Straight: Edison Lighthouse and the inventor.)

(19) TREAT (Endless agreement = TREAT-Y; to pay for someone is to treat them.)

(20) LARK (Single Cryptic.)

(22) FILTH (Double Straight.)

(23) STEM (Rising clue.)

No. 5

ACROSS

(1) Mixed peach is a real bargain. (5)
(5) She's nothing but looked up to. (4)
(8) Sounds like requirements to prepare bread. (5)
(9) Salesman told untruths but returned the call. (7)
(10) Marched out then won over. (7)
(11) I hear this woman's never happy. (4)
(12) This will be required for the hearing. (3)
(14) Skylight? (4)
(15) Part of the mural sold as well. (4)
(18) Initially Kenyan Impala Tribes will get equipment. (3)
(21) Sort of printing. (4)
(23) Poster one can reveal will give fencing stroke. (7)
(25) An all round coach? (7)
(26) Special gift to administer cure. (5)

(27) Man with a split personality. (4)
(28) Inquisitive, definitely not, backward OK. (5)

DOWN

(1) They just won't believe it. (6)
(2) The Spanish man's a gent sort of charming. (7)
(3) It tells you when and where it came from. (8)
(4) One in business gave long abusive speech. (6)
(5) There's still a chance to meet an old comedian. (4)
(6) One horn! That's strange, it has. (5)
(7) Quick identification of brewed ale, perfect. (5)
(13) Crazy red monk. (8)
(16) Close relations were nurses. (7)
(17) Those will give spirit to the people. (5)
(19) Ford model is corroded but reliable. (6)
(20) Very good man inside the church room. (6)
(22) Write to New York for money. (5)
(24) The seaman the French feel are qualified. (4)

Answers to Crossword No. 5
ACROSS

(1) CHEAP (Anagram of PEACH.)

(5) HERO (She's = HER; nothing = O; a hero is looked up to.)

(8) NEEDS (Sounds Like clue: kneads is what a breadmaker does.)

(9) REPLIED (Salesman = REP; told untruths = LIED; Straight clue: returned call.)

(10) CHARMED (Anagram of MARCHED, indicated by the word 'out'.)

(11) MONA (Sounds Like clue: the woman sounds like a 'moaner'.)

(12) EAR (Single Cryptic clue.)

(14) STAR (Single Cryptic.)

(15) ALSO (Word From Two Words clue, indicated by the words 'part of': Straight clue: as well.)

(18) KIT (Initial clue.)

(21) TYPE (Double Straight.)

(23) RIPOSTE (Anagram of POSTER and a 'I', indicated by reveal; Straight clue: fencing stroke.)

(25) OMNIBUS (Extra Cryptic Single Cryptic: all round = OMNI, Coach = BUS; an Omnibus takes one all round.)

(26) TREAT (Double Straight.)

(27) HYDE (Single Cryptic.)

(28) NOSEY (Straight Clue: Inquisitive; definitely not = NO; OK = YES, but backwards = SEY.)

DOWN

(1) CYNICS (Single Cryptic.)

(2) ELEGANT (Abbreviation of the Spanish man = EL; Anagram indicated by 'sort of', A GENT.)

(3) POSTMARK (Single Cryptic, a little straight.)

(4) TIRADE (One = I; in indicates 'inside''; business = TRADE. A tirade is a flow of abuse.)

(5) HOPE (Double Straight: chance is obvious; the comedian is Bob Hope.)

(6) RHINO (One = I; Anagram of 'horn' indicated by 'that's strange'; Cryptic 'it has'.)

(7) IDEAL (The word 'quick' can mean an Abbreviation. Abbreviation of identification = ID; Anagram of ale, indicated by 'brewed'; Straight clue: perfect.)

(13) RASPUTIN (Single Cryptic: red = Russian). Mad Russian Monk who had great influence over the wife of Tsar Nicholas II.

(16)   SISTERS (Double Straight.)
(17)   ETHOS (Anagram of THOSE, indicated by 'will give'. Ethos is character or spirit.)
(19)   TRUSTY (Ford model = T; corroded = RUSTY.)
(20)   VESTRY (VERY, Whole Word; Abbreviation of good man = ST; inside = inside VE..RY; Straight clue: church room.)
(22)   PENNY (Write to = PEN; Abbreviation of New York = NY.)
(24)   ABLE (Abbreviation of seaman = AB; the French = LE; Straight clue: qualified.)

No. 6

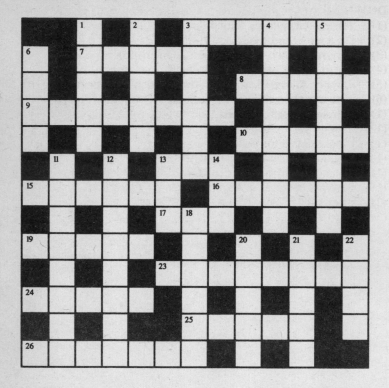

ACROSS

(3)   1,000 now pop. (7)
(7)   Distant religion that's absurd. (5)
(8)   A bird is concealed in jumbled pines. (5)
(9)   Before nurses one imagines. (8)
(10) Revolting red. (5)
(13) Queen for a generation. (3)
(15) See 24 Across.
(16) The plain situation is holding it in place. (2,4)
(17) That's strange, it's not even. (3)
(19) One tune that will make people come together. (5)
(23) You'll end up here if you take too much bread. (2,3,3)
(24 & 15 Ac) Demand to suspend a sentence? (5,2,4)
(25) Got bored with not getting sleep. (5)
(26) Before Dick, he's a real marksman. (7)

DOWN

(1)   The Queen follows behind later on. (5)

(2)   Defer order to be released. (5)

(3)   Give info to the German regarding sex. (6)

(4)   No six points, what poppycock. (8)

(5)   Initially Alan Parker shows the way to take someone on. (8)

(6)   Measure and record. (4)

(11) Released after birth and made film of it. (4,4)

(12) You'll find a crow's nest up here. (8)

(13) Eastern leave for yourself. (3)

(14) A little identification may be a help. (3)

(18) Donald had his feed, now make a contribution. (6)

(20) Southern musical instrument tuned by a key. (5)

(21) Swap the business. (5)

(22) Rewrite diet. (4)

Answers to Crossword No. 6

ACROSS

(3)   GRANDAD (1,000 = GRAND; now = AD; Straight clue: pop.)

(7)   FARCE (Distant = FAR; Religion = CE, Church of England Abbreviation; Straight clue: absurd.)

(8)   SNIPE (Anagram of PINES, indicated by 'jumbled'; Straight clue: a bird.)

(9)   PRETENDS (Before = PRE; nurses = TENDS; Straight clue: imagines.)

(10) LENIN (Double Meaning Word: red means Russian.)

(13) ERA (Queen = ER; Whole Word = A; Straight clue: a generation.)

(15) See 24 Ac.

(16) IN SITU (Word From Two Words clue, indicated by 'holding'; Straight clue: in place.)

(17) ODD (Double Straight.)

(19) UNITE (One = I; Anagram of TUNE, indicated by 'that will make'; Straight clue: come together.)

(23) IN THE RED (Double Meaning clue: bread meaning money, not food.)

(24 & 15 Ac) ORDER TO HANG (Single Cryptic using a Double Meaning clue.)

(25) TIRED (Double Straight clue.)

(26) DEADEYE (Cryptic: put deadeye before Dick and you have a marksman.)

DOWN

(1)   AFTER (Queen = ER; 'follows' means it follows the next clue; behind = AFT; Straight clue: later on.)

(2)   FREED (Anagram of DEFER, indicated by 'order'.)

(3)   GENDER (Give info = GEN; 'the' in German = DER; Straight clue: sex.)

(4)   NONSENSE (Whole Word clue: NO; six points = N-S-E-N-S-E; Straight clue: poppycock.)

(5)   APPOINTS (Initials clue: A-lan P-arker; shows the way = POINTS; Straight clue: take someone on.)

(6)   TAPE (Double Meaning clue.)

(11) BORN FREE (Release = FREE; the word 'after' indicates that it should be put after the next clue; birth = BORN; Straight clue: film.)

(12) MASTHEAD (Double Meaning Word: you could assume I meant a bird's nest.)

(13) EGO (Eastern = E; Leave = GO; Straight clue: yourself.)

(14) AID (A, Whole Word; little identification = ID; Straight clue: a help.)

(18) DONATE (Donald = DON; had his feed = ATE; Straight clue: make a contribution.)

(20) SHARP (Southern = S; musical instrument = HARP; Straight clue: a key.)

(21) TRADE (Double Straight.)

(22) EDIT (A nice concise Cryptic clue. The word 'rewrite' has a double purpose here: it is a Straight clue as well as an indication that the word DIET is an Anagram.)

No. 7

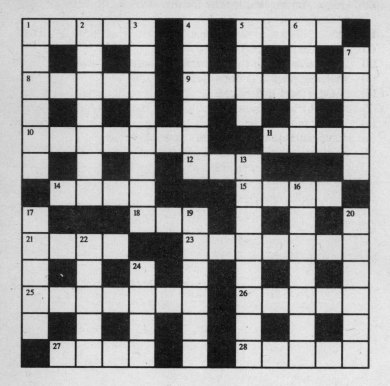

ACROSS

(1) Pull the Spaniard in to dry. (5)

(5) Twisted lips may give sound so. (4)

(8) Caesar's words. (5)

(9) Fun was over when finished drawing. (4,3)

(10) That's one fib too many so stay in bed. (7)

(11) Before untangling a net. (4)

(12) Got a nervous twitch when hearing it's approved. (3)

(14) American Queen has a drug problem. (4)

(15) Behold School exercising can be a big step. (4)

(18) Low light to see small measurement. (3)

(21) Initially Theatrical Union twice presented ballet piece. (4)

(23) Flower for the Womble. (7)

(25) Jacques Cousteau's favourite song? (7)

(26) Signature tune from the Meeting Place. (5)

(27) Half of the grownups returned then went round. (4)

(28) Hose attachments for the flowers. (5)

DOWN

(1) The candlemaker is fat. (6)

(2) Overlook having to give endorsement. (7)

(3) A letter from a country Nobleman. (8)

(4) Engine part that sounds as though we should give it a small rap. (6)

(5) Jack's missus won't have it. (4)

(6) The exhibition up north has gone. (5)

(7) It's not on, the queen made a bid. (5)

(13) Costlier sort of convent. (8)

(16) Ability to make nothing of a point in the papers. (7)

(17) Got a pile for the chimney. (5)

(19) Feeling gloomy as the extra large are coming in more. (6)

(20) Properties for monopoly. (6)

(22) Put up around fifty one to flower. (5)

(24) Reveal nothing to a writer. (4)

Answers to Crossword No. 7

ACROSS

(1)   TOWEL (Pull = TOW; the Spaniard = EL; Straight clue: to dry.)

(5)   LISP (Anagram of LIPS indicated by 'twisted'.)

(8)   LATIN (Single Cryptic: Caesar spoke Latin.)

(9)   PLAY OFF (Straightish first clue, Double Meaning word "Drawing". Another example of bad English to confuse. It should be a draw, or drew.)

(10) OVERLIE (Cryptic first part; Straight clue: stay in bed.)

(11) ANTE (Anagram of A NET, indicated by 'untangling'; Straight clue: before.)

(12) TIC (Sounds Like clue; sounds like a tick.)

(14) USER (Two Abbreviations: American = US, Queen = ER; a person with a drug problem is a USER.)

(15) LOPE (Behold = LO, as in lo and behold; school exercises = PE; Straight clue: Big step.)

(18) DIM (A low light can be a dim light; small measurement = Abbreviaton of DIMensions.)

(21) TUTU (Initials clue: TU twice; Straightish clue: ballet piece.)

(23) ORINOCO (Double Meaning clue: Flower = River, as in the Orinoco river; one of the Wombles was called Orinoco.)

(25) CALYPSO (The ship of Jacques Cousteau, the famous diver, is called Calypso.)

(26) THEME (Word From Two Words clue.)

(27) SPUN (Literally half of GrowNUPS; returned, means reverse.)

(28) ROSES (Double Straight clue.)

DOWN

(1)   TALLOW (Double Straight: among other things, the fat tallow was used for candlemaking.)

(2)   WITNESS (Double Straight clue.)

(3)   LANDLORD (Straight clue: a letter, a landlord 'lets'; Country = LAND; Nobleman = LORD.)

(4)   TAPPET (A Sounds Like clue: sounds like 'tap it'.)

(5)   LEAN (Single Cryptic: Jack Spratt will eat no fat, etc., etc.)

(6)   SHOWN (Word Exchange of exhibition = SHOW; Abbreviation of N-orth; Straight clue: has gone.)

(7)   OFFER (Not on = OFF; the Queen = ER; Straight clue: made a bid.)

(13) CLOISTER (Anagram of COSTLIER, indicated by 'sort'; another word for convent is cloister.)

(16) PROWESS (Nothing = O; Point = W; 'in' means insert in the papers = PRESS.)

(17) STACK (Double Straight.)

(19) MOROSE (Extra large = OS, Abbreviation of Outsize; 'coming in' another phrase for insert; Whole Word MOR--E.)

(20) HOTELS (Monopoly as in the board game, not its literal meaning.)

(22) TULIP (put 'up' = TUP; 'around' indicates wrapping around fifty one = LI; TU-LI-P.)

(24) OPEN (Nothing = O; Writer = PEN; to open is to reveal.)

No. 8

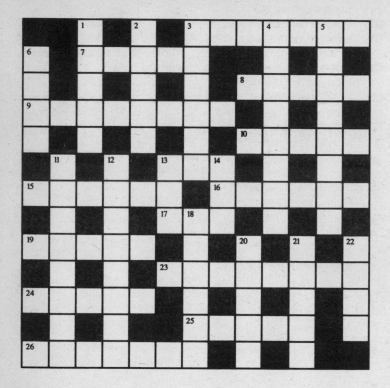

ACROSS

(3)   All points to him to give information. (7)
(7)   German flower. (5)
(8)   Opening style will get reward it's said. (5)
(9)   A letter I distributed to show I am educated. (8)
(10)   A case for brains? (5)
(13)   Three pieces of Pear could complement a meal. (3)
(15)   You must be armed to enter here. (6)
(16)   Making returns was not his speciality. (6)
(17)   With endless acumen. (3)
(19)   Agitate, then remove it, to uncover stone. (5)
(23)   The Admiral spoke well enough to make plenty of money. (8)
(24)   The man mixed gin inside, to make it swing. (5)
(25)   Country for farmers. (5)
(26)   Vision a roller. (7)

DOWN

(1) I speed, that's mad. (5)
(2) Heard crying in several rows. (5)
(3) In the home for lovers the French cuddle up. (6)
(4) Hands out punishment. (8)
(5) Total tribute was heard from sailor. (8)
(6) Paperwork required to release prisoner? (4)
(11) Would a garden pest feel so after a long crawl? (8)
(12) Writer had to join crowd to see American building. (8)
(13) Seat for a quiet bet. (3)
(14) Pretend it's the law. (3)
(18) In the company, even though he's ailing. (6)
(20) Student in gory surround got honour. (5)
(21) Males turned away food. (5)
(22) Either way it's still a name. (4)

Answers to Crossword No. 8

ACROSS

(3) NEWSMAN (All points = N-E-W-S; him = MAN; who gives information.)

(7) RHINE (You will remember 'flower' can be a river as on page 36, which makes this a very easy clue.)

(8) PRISE (A Sounds Like clue: it sounds like prize, indicated by 'it's said'; Straight clue: opening style.)

(9) LITERATE (Anagram of A-LETTER-I, indicated by 'distributed'.)

(10) SKULL (Single Cryptic.)

(13) PEA (Three pieces of pear = PEA-R.)

(15) SLEEVE (Single Cryptic.)

(16) CANUTE (Single Cryptic: as in King Canute's inability to make the tide return.)

(17) WIT ('Endless' means remove last letter of WIT-H; acumen is a type of wit, as in sharpness not humour.)

(19) AGATE (Remove 'it' from AG-IT-ATE.)

(23) AFFLUENT (Admiral = AF, Abbreviation of Admiral of the Fleet; spoke well = FLUENT.)

(24) HINGE (The man = HE; an Anagram of GIN, indicated by 'mixed'; inside H-ING-E.)

(25) RURAL (Single Cryptic, unless of course you related the word 'country' to countryside not 'a' country, in which case it's a straight clue.)

(26) PHANTOM (Double Straight clue, as in a Rolls Royce Phantom.)

DOWN

(1) IRATE (Whole Word I; speed = RATE; Straight clue: mad.)

(2) TIERS (A Sounds Like clue indicated by 'heard': crying = tears; Straight clue: several rows. This clue also incorporated the Double Meaning deception: you were led to believe, because of the word crying, that the word 'row' meant an argument not a line.)

(3) NESTLE (Lovers' home = NEST; the French = LE; Straight clue: cuddle up.)

(4) STRIKING (Double Cryptic: Hands being workers.)

(5) ABSOLUTE (Sounds Like clue: Sailor = AB, tribute = SALUTE.)

(6) FILE (Single Cryptic.)

(11) SLUGGISH (Single Cryptic.) (A nice clue.)

(12) PENTAGON (Writer = PEN; join crowd = TAG ON.)

(13) PEW (Quiet = P; a bet = EW, abbreviation of Each Way.)

(14) ACT (Double Straight.)

(18) INFIRM (Whole Word: IN; the company = FIRM; Straight clue: ailing.)

(20) GLORY (Abbreviation of student = L, in g-ory surrounding.)

(21) MEALS (Anagram of MALES indicated by 'turned'.)

(22) OTTO (Either way means it can be read both ways.)

No. 9

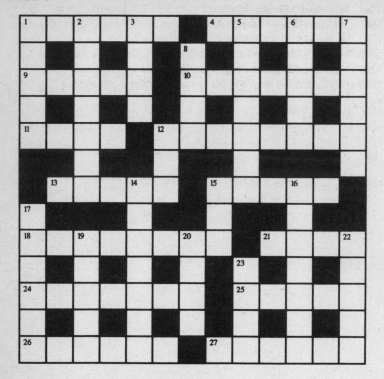

ACROSS

(1)   The French mark sailor. (6)
(4)   Heard a singer's note. (6)
(9)   Type of burn? (5)
(10) A watch with fingers not hands? (7)
(11) Track that leads to section of Motorway. (4)
(12) Brains e.g. will give an idea of direction. (8)
(13) No charge to five hundred, it's been released. (5)
(15) Closes a circus act. (5)
(18) Tars area of ground for modern art. (8)
(21) Southern resting place for a Celt. (4)
(24) The eastern Claret when stirred is very sweet and sticky. (7)
(25) Right in temporary shelter by the river. (5)
(26) Dirges turned on hills. (6)
(27) No scope to find fruit. (6)

DOWN

(1) Science room the Spaniard may use for identification. (5)
(2) You'll turn nuts if you use it. (7)
(3) Give support to the east, he will assist. (4)
(5) Direction George turned to devour with greed. (7)
(6) Underweight, this is really off. (3,2)
(7) Enjoy the sauce. (6)
(8) Lied around doing nothing. (4)
(12) It's not good for the fish to rise. (3)
(14) A listener's complaint. (7)
(15) Took exam on short day. (3)
(16) Father could read from it. (7)
(17) Substance that's a concern. (6)
(19) Deep south coming up fast. (5)
(20) I removed the chief cook. (4)
(22) Book name for the Championship. (5)
(23) Turn round and cause trouble. (4)

Answers to Crossword No. 9
ACROSS
(1)   LASCAR (The French = LA; mark = SCAR. A Lascar is an old term for a sailor.)

(4)   TENNER (Sounds Like clue: singer = TENOR; a TENNER is a banknote.)

(9)   BRAND (Double Meaning clue: a type may be a BRAND, to burn may be to brand.)

(10)   DIGITAL (Single Cryptic: Fingers are Digits.)

(11)   LANE (Double Straight.)

(12)   BEARINGS (Anagram of BRAINS E.G. indicated by 'will give'; Straight clue: direction.)

(13)   FREED (No charge = FREE; 500 = D: Straight clue: released.)

(15)   SEALS (Double Straight.)

(18)   ABSTRACT (Tars = ABS, plural of sailors; Area of ground = TRACT.)

(21)   SCOT (Southern = S; resting place = COT.)

(24)   TREACLE (Eastern = E; Anagram of CLARET, indicated by 'when stirred'.)

(25)   TRENT (Right = R; temporary shelter = TENT.)

(26)   RIDGES (Anagram of DIRGES, indicated by 'turned'; you can find ridges on hills.)

(27)   ORANGE (No = O; Scope = RANGE.)

DOWN
(1)   LABEL (Science room = LAB; the Spaniard = EL.)

(2)   SPANNER (Double Meaning Word clue. The sentence was worded to sound as though you would go mad.)

(3)   AIDE (Support = AID; east = E; Straight clue: he will assist.)

(5)   ENGORGE (Direction = N E S or W, in this case N is required, which is put with GEORGE for an Anagram indicated by 'turned'.)

(6)   NOT ON (Cryptic first section: underweight = NO TON; followed by the straight clue.)

(7)   RELISH (Double Straight.)

(8)   IDLE (Anagram of LIED indicated by 'around'; Straight clue: doing nothing.)

(12)   BAD (fish = DAB, rising = BAD.)

(14)   EARACHE (Listener = EAR.)

(15)   SAT (Straight clue: took exam; Abbreviation: short day = SAT.)

(16) LECTERN (Double Meaning: father as in person of the Church.)

(17) MATTER (Double Meaning clue.)

(19) SPEED (Whole Word: DEEP; South = S; coming up means reverse the word in a 'Down clue' = S-PEED.)

(20) CHEF ('I removed' means literally remove the I from chief.)

(22) TITLE (Double Straight.)

(23) STIR (Double Straight. If you stir tea you turn it round.)

No. 10

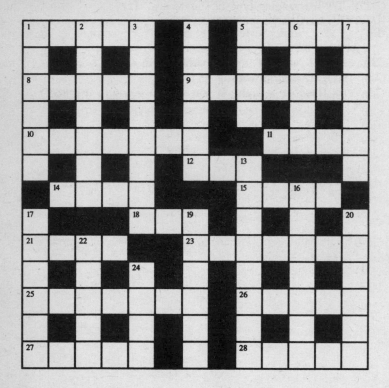

ACROSS

(1) The middle man in the nursery. (5)

(5) Positions at the end of the barrel we hear. (5)

(8) 1 man sells them or may drive one. (5)

(9) Foul man? (7)

(10) Position Phoenix? (7)

(11) Turning circle for a swimmer. (4)

(12) Head banger? (3)

(14) Is again a goddess. (4)

(15) It's a beautiful place to wander round it's said. (4)

(18) The last word in pictures? (3)

(21) Force head off! Barmy. (4)

(23) About a hundred and fifty one points laid out. (7)

(25) Initially Public Relations Officer Mr. Crosby was very in depth. (7)

(26) Decoration when one's below. (5)
(27) Try rearranging type of square seat. (5)
(28) Replaced large music maker. (5)

DOWN
(1) Alcohol supplier has prohibition to carry gun. (6)
(2) Measures to take when it's extremely cold. (7)
(3) About the odds on points, should get a reaction. (8)
(4) I say thanks to Scot for renewing my drive. (6)
(5) So short distance and very quiet. (4)
(6) Shaky roots to the trunk. (5)
(7) Wizard times? (6)
(13) Rehearsal custom. (8)
(16) Chinese girl joined post. (7)
(17) Transport favourite covering. (6)
(19) A mythical animal but sounds as though it will last a long time. (6)
(20) Right after this side of the road will come to Church Warden. (6)
(22) Southern room erected on wasteland. (5)
(24) There's no more rounds. (4)

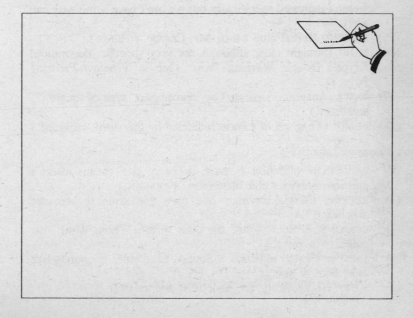

Answers to Crossword No. 10

ACROSS

(1) BAKER (Single Cryptic: the Butcher, the Baker and the Candlestick Maker, etc.)

(5) SITES (A Sounds Like clue: it sounds like the sights on a rifle.)

(8) ROLLS (Single Cryptic: '1 man' means 1 Across, who is a Baker.)

(9) REFEREE (Single Cryptic.) When a compiler sets the clues, occasionally one emerges that gives him a great deal of pleasure. This one did for me. Sorry.

(10) ARIZONA (Single Cryptic.)

(11) POOL ('Turning' means reversing the letters or word; LOOP = POOL.)

(12) CAP (Single Cryptic: a cap is an explosive device.)

(14) ISIS (IS again = repeat; Straight clue: a goddess.)

(15) ROME (Sounds Like clue: Rome sounds like roam.)

(18) END (Single Cryptic with a Double Meaning Word, pictures. It's intended that you think I mean pictures as in paintings.)

(21) ARMY (Straight clue first: force; head off means remove the first letter (B)ARMY.)

(23) RECLINE (A many part clue: about = RE; a hundred = C; fifty = L; one = I; points in the plural = NE − of course, these weren't indicated specifically but we can't have it too easy can we?)

(25) PROBING (Initial clue P-R-O; Mr. Crosby = BING.)

(26) ICING (Straight clue, although not very specific: decoration; Cryptic Double Meaning Word: One = 1 below Freezing Point.)

(27) TASTE (Anagram, indicated by 'rearranging' type of square (T) and SEAT.)

(28) ELGAR (Anagram of LARGE indicated by the word 'replaced'.)

DOWN

(1) BARMAN (Prohibition = BAN; 'to carry gun' means insert a gun into previous clue answer = B-ARM-AN.)

(2) KELVINS (Single Cryptic: one uses this scale to measure absolute 0°.)

(3) RESPONSE (About = RE; the odds = SP; Whole Word: ON; points = S and E.)

(4) TARMAC ('I say' indicates a Sounds Like clue: ta sounds like TAR; Scot = MAC.)

(5) SOFT (Whole Word: SO; short distance = FT.)

(6) TORSO (Anagram of ROOTS indicated by 'shaky'.)

(7) SPELLS (Single Cryptic.)

(13) PRACTICE (Double Straight clue.)

(16) MAILING (A difficult clue: Chinese girl = MAI LING; 'joined' means make one word.)

(17) CARPET (Transport = CAR; favourite = PET.)

(19) DRAGON (Sounds Like clue: DRAG-ON.)

(20) VERGER (Right = R after VERGE.)

(22) MOORS (Southern = S; ROOM 'erected' means write upwards from the bottom of the grid.)

(24) TIME (Single Cryptic: rounds has several meanings. Here it means pub rounds.)

No. 11

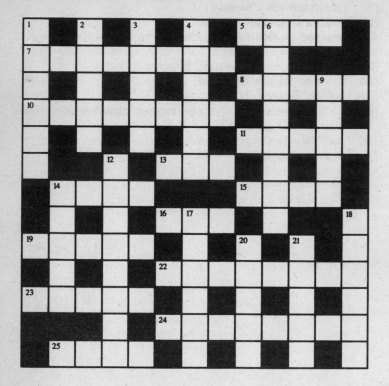

ACROSS

(5) Nemo returned to give warning. (4)
(7) Opening words in the post? (4,4)
(8) It's apparent it will be seen through. (5)
(10) Accounts for the docks. (8)
(11) Delay in the market place. (5)
(13) Remove the snake from here as soon as possible. (3)
(14) The swine is late. (4)
(15) I fled to the country. (4)
(16) Could be a perfect container for grass. (3)
(19) A way the queen gives the daisy. (5)
(22) See 12 down.
(23) Stable lad's wife? (5)
(24) Resistance to create irritation. (8)
(25) The real gent is almost a sweetie. (4)

DOWN

(1)   A time and place to unite. (6)

(2)   The dog is terrified of water. (5)

(3)   American woman who shows the way. (5)

(4)   Take me away from these cuddles and caresses, even though I need them for support. (6)

(6)   Man who has the 'force'. (8)

(9)   Gathered together and exhausted. (3,2)

(12 & 22 Ac)   Not an alien but a green man who likes our planet. (6,2,3,5)

(14)   Model of quiet large Queen. (5)

(17)   Headless parents and all the rest. (6)

(18)   We hear a monarch could be in pain. (6)

(20)   Seat for the magistrate. (5)

(21)   When it goes against this it's very annoying. (5)

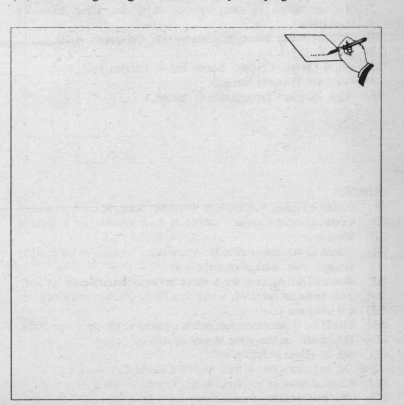

Answers to Crossword No. 11

ACROSS

(5)   OMEN (Nemo returned means exactly that.)

(7)   DEAR SIRS (Single Cryptic. A little chauvinistic perhaps but it does fit the grid.)

(8)   CLEAR (Double Straight clue.)

(10) EVIDENCE (Double Meaning Word, docks.)

(11) STALL (Double Straight clue.)

(13) ASP (Word From Two Words, indicated by 'from'.)

(14) PORK (Single Cryptic using a Double Meaning Word, swine, to confuse; 'swine' is meant in its literal sense, not as an expletive; 'late' also means dead, so we are left with dead pig.)

(15) IRAN (Whole Word 'I'; fled = RAN; Straight clue: country.)

(16) POT (Single Cryptic using Double Meaning Word 'grass' to confuse again. In this instance it is the slang term for marijuana.)

(19) ASTER (Whole Word 'A'; Way = ST; the queen = ER.)

(22) (See 12 Down.)

(23) BRIDE (Single Cryptic: Stable lad = Groom.)

(24) FRICTION (Double Straight.)

(25) TOFF (Single Cryptic: almost 'toffee'.)

DOWN

(1)   ADHERE (Time = AD; place = HERE; Straight clue: to unite.)

(2)   RABID (Single Cryptic: rabies is hydrophobia or a fear of water.)

(3)   USHER (Two Abbreviations: American / woman = US & HER; Straight clue: who shows the way.)

(4)   BRACES (A long clue for a short answer. Simply take 'M & E' away from em-BRACES, which is a Word Exchange for cuddles and caresses.)

(6)   MILITARY (Single Cryptic. It has nothing to do with Star Wars. The 'force' in this case is any of the services.)

(9)   ALL IN (Double Straight.)

(12 & 22 Ac) FRIEND OF THE EARTH (Single Cryptic.)

(14) POSER (Quiet = P; large = OS, Queen = ER.)

(17) OTHERS (Headless means remove the first letter of M-OTHERS.)

(18) ACHING (Sounds Like clue indicated by 'sounds like', A KING.)

(20) BENCH (Single Cryptic, dangerously straight.)

(21) GRAIN (Single Cryptic: as in the saying "It goes against the grain".)

No. 12

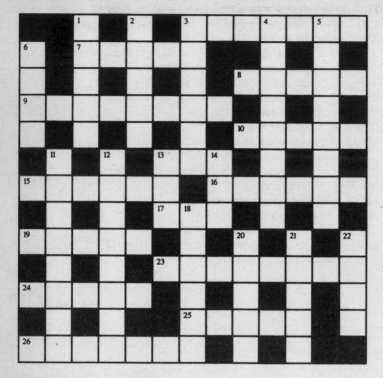

ACROSS

(3) What's left can be put down. (7)
(7) Do use it all to put out the fire. (5)
(8) A second behind him. (5)
(9) Were sick, you and I coming to a headless lion, must have been a trick. (8)
(10) To scorch is a crime and a backward example. (5)
(13) A general reversal of a swimmer. (3)
(15) 50% of the SS? (6)
(16) Type of glue used for fixing a post. (6)
(17) Got the goat sonny? (3)
(19) Rock star? (5)
(23) A varying tiny diet for the personality. (8)
(24) Put a large number on the shelf pop...... (5)
(25) ......and another on its own for a copy. (5)
(26) About the poem, take it back. (7)

DOWN

(1) Although one may sound like an idiot, they're actually quite mature. (5)

(2) Swear for a spell. (5)

(3) Initially the Department of the Environment has a show of hands to commit themselves entirely. (6)

(4) Shake rag in oil, well that's new. (8)

(5) A gin is in, now sort out the coat of arms. (8)

(6) Complain about the copy. (4)

(11) Music for the night workers. (8)

(12) I yearn to be taken around odd Scottish family, that's the point. (8)

(13) The largest deer comes from Correl Kreek. (3)

(14) A boy born fifty years after Christ. (3)

(18) The way to bring on late starter. (6)

(20) Last words after a breakdown? (2,3)

(21) Get down from here. (5)

(22) Sounds like a vote in favour for viewing. (4)

Answers to Crossword No. 12

ACROSS

(3)   DEPOSIT (Double Straight clue.)

(7)   DOUSE (Word From Two Words: DO-USE.)

(8)   FIRST (Double Meaning clue: a 'second' refers to second place, not the increment of time.)

(9)   ILLUSION (Word Exchanging clue: Sick = ILL, you and I = US; headless lion = L-ION.)

(10) SINGE (Word Exchange: crime = SIN; backward example = GE.)

(13) EEL (Double Meaning Word: 'general', General LEE reversed gives a swimmer.)

(15) SOCIAL (Single Cryptic: 50% of Social Security.)

(16) ARABIC (Double Meaning of the word 'post' incorporating the 'bad English' element. Arabic gum is used to seal letters.)

(17) KID (Double Straight.)

(19) STONE (Single Cryptic: as in a Rolling Stone.)

(23) IDENTITY (Anagram of TINY DIET indicated by 'varying'.)

(24) CRACK (Abbreviation of large number = C; Word Exchange: shelf = RACK; Straight clue: pop.)

(25) CLONE (Continuation lines pertain to another large number = C; on its own = LONE; Straight clue: a copy.)

(26) REVERSE (Abbreviation: about = RE; Word Exchange: poem = VERSE; Straight clue: take it back.)

DOWN

(1)   ADULT (Sounds Like clue: A DOLT.)

(2)   CURSE (Double Straight clue.)

(3)   DEVOTE (Initials clue: DE; show of hands = VOTE.)

(4)   ORIGINAL (Anagram of RAG IN OIL, indicated by 'shake'.)

(5)   INSIGNIA (Anagram of A GIN IS IN, indicated by 'now sort out'; Straight clue: a coat of arms.)

(6)   CRIB (Double Straight clue.)

(11) NOCTURNE (Double Straight, although a little obscure: night music and a nocturnal animal are both Nocturnes.)

(12) PINNACLE (Word Exchange: Yearn = PINE; wrap around an Anagram of CLAN, indicated by 'odd'; Straight clue: the point.)

(13) ELK (Word From Two Words clue.)

(14) LAD (Abbreviations of fifty = L, years after Christ = AD.)

(18) INDUCE (Double Meaning clue of the words 'late starter'. The answer is a method to advance childbirth.)

(20) ON-TOW (Single Cryptic. I liked this one.)

(21) EIDER (Double Meaning word: down meant Duck feathers not a descent.)

(22) EYES (Sounds Like clue: a vote in favour = 'ayes'.)

No. 13

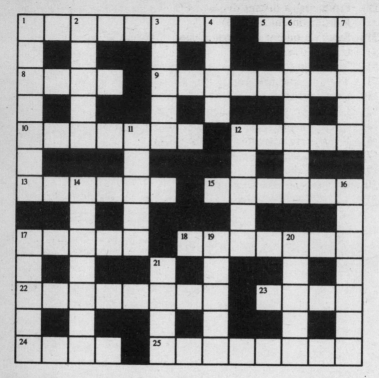

ACROSS

- (1) What to do on laundry day to freshen up. (8)
- (5) Assist with what the punter does. (4)
- (8) Ketch's tool. (4)
- (9) Steam in a tumbler will move it. (8)
- (10) One gravity communist took no notice of. (7)
- (12) Stick that is to say for the boy. (5)
- (13) He takes stock at the end of the barrel. (6)
- (15) First director? (6)
- (17) Benefit from a personal problem in north America. (5)
- (18) Square up before excuse for crime. (7)
- (22) Lost one's cool after the big bang. (8)
- (23) A. Barker's usual name.... (4)
- (24) ....name change on the horse. (4)
- (25) What Phoebe gives. (3,2,3)

DOWN

(1) Producing a distant dynasty. (7)

(2) Put top on chicken. (5)

(3) Surprise one at Hampton Court. (5)

(4) Come down hard. (4)

(6) You're up the wall mate to play cricket. (7)

(7) Try the state new route. (5)

(11) Come up to point stag to plants round water. (5)

(12) Extraction I hear even tennis players use. (5)

(14) There's actually ten but you wouldn't think so. (7)

(16) Felt poorly after the accident. (3,4)

(17) The fish came right in the light. (5)

(19) Flippin' shade! (5)

(20) Roll for the countryman. (5)

(21) Now! You are saying we should go to Sussex Valley. (4)

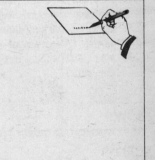

Answers to Crossword No. 13
ACROSS
(1)   FACEWASH (Laundry day = FACE the WASH.)

(5)   ABET (As in to aid and ABET; the punter has A BET.)

(8)   ROPE (Jack Ketch is a hangman, his main tool is a ROPE.)

(9)   ANIMATES (Anagram of STEAM IN A, 'tumbler' indicates an anagram.)

(10) IGNORED (One = I; gravity = G; communist took no = NO RED.)

(12) JAMIE (Stick = JAM; that is to say = IE; boy = JAMIE.)

(13) GUNNER (Double Meaning Words 'stock' and 'barrel'.)

(15) WINNER (Double Straight: first = WINNER, the film director Michael WINNER.)

(17) BONUS (Straight clue: 'benefit'; personal problem = BO; north America = N US.)

(18) TREASON (Square = T; excuse = REASON.)

(22) EXPLODED (Double Straight: you 'explode' if you lose your temper.)

(23) FIDO (A barker means a dog.)

(24) MANE (Anagram of NAME.)

(25) RAY OF SUN (Single Cryptic: Phoebe is an affectionate term for the sun.)

DOWN
(1)   FARMING (Straight clue: producing; distant = FAR; dynasty = MING.)

(2)   CAPON (Top = CAP; Whole Word = ON: Straight clue: chicken.)

(3)   AMAZE (Straight clue: surprise; at Hampton Court there is A MAZE.)

(4)   HAIL (Single Cryptic: as in a HAILstorm.)

(6)   BATSMAN (Up the wall = BATS; mate = MAN.)

(7)   TASTE (Anagram of STATE; Straight clue: 'try'.)

(11) REEDS (Point = S; stag = DEER; coming up = REEDS.)

(12) JUICE (Straight clue: extraction = JUICE; Sounds Like clue: to be 40 all in points in tennis = DEUCE.)

(14) NINEPIN (Single Cryptic: the game NINEPINS actually has ten pins.)

(16) RUN DOWN (Single Cryptic. Too obvious to explain.)

(17) BREAM (Right = R; in the light = B-EAM.)

(19) RUDDY (Double Straight clue: flippin' = ruddy; ruddy is also a shade.)

(20) SWISS (Double Straight.)

(21) ADUR (Now = AD; Sounds Like clue: you are = UR.)

No. 14

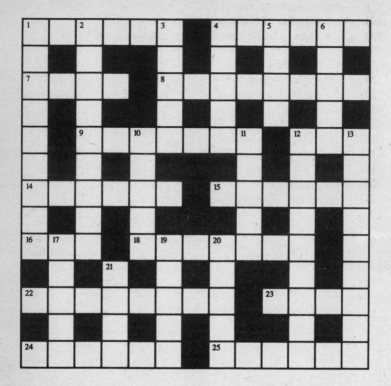

ACROSS

(1) A leap forward in large number. (6)
(4) Hat to wear for cricket? (6)
(7) Little knowledge? (4)
(8) Was Teri skilled with part of star? (8)
(9) Leaving the division. (7)
(12) Grasp part of the crawler. (3)
(14) Fools the dictator to turn south. (6)
(15) Carrier of liquor that's to say. (6)
(16) An early bird. (3)
(18) They can pull strings and break the rules at an auction. (7)
(22) Complain about the volume of the radio? (5,3)
(23) Left the harbour. (4)
(24) Metal covers for the food. (6)
(25) Right, now follow the supporter. (6)

DOWN

(1) Large cut of the action. (1,3,5)
(2) Leaving after the winter to find my kid. (9)
(3) First type to pull in men. (5)
(4) Keep on going give stick. (5)
(5) The new artist revealed a blemish. (4)
(6) What aspirin does gently. (5)
(10) It spins both ways. (5)
(11) He's forever sitting with a fishing rod. (5)
(12) One southern wine to take racing. (9)
(13) Outside each one has a recorder. (9)
(17) Low sound to raise scholar. (5)
(19) I sold out of Icons (5)
(20) Pick attack. (2,3)
(21) Rate of travelling in the main. (4)

Answers to Crossword No. 14

ACROSS

(1)   ABOUND (A leap = A BOUND.)

(4)   BOWLER (Single Cryptic.)

(7)   INFO (A little INFOrmation.)

(8)   ASTERISK (Word From Two Words: wAS TERI SKilled.)

(9)   PARTING (Double Straight.)

(12) ASP (Word From Two Words, in this particular clue, one: grASP.)

(14) IDIOTS (The dictator = IDI Amin; 'to' turn = OT; south = S.)

(15) PORTER (Single Cryptic.)

(16) EGG (Single Cryptic.)

(18) RINGERS (BellRINGERS pull strings; a system at the auction to purchase lots cheaply is called ringing.)

(22) SOUND OFF (Single Cryptic.)

(23) PORT (Left = PORT; harbour = PORT.)

(24) PLATES (To coat with metal is to PLATE.)

(25) RAFTER (Right = R; Follow = AFTER.)

DOWN

(1)   A BIG SLICE (Single Cryptic, dangerously close to a Straight clue.)

(2)   OFFSPRING (leaving = OFF; SPRING follows winter.)

(3)   DRAFT (Double Straight: first type is a DRAFT, to force men to join = DRAFT.)

(4)   BATON (Keep on = BAT ON.)

(5)   WART (neW ARTist.)

(6)   EASES (Double Straight.)

(10) ROTOR (Palindrome: i.e. ROTOR reads both ways.)

(11) GNOME (A common garden gnome has a fishing rod.)

(12) AUTOSPORT (One = AUTO; southern = S; wine = PORT.)

(13) PERIMETER (Each one = PER; One = I; recorder = METER.)

(17) GROWL (Raise = GROW; scholar = L.)

(19) IDOLS (Anagram of 'I sold'. An Icon can be an idol.)

(20) GO FOR (Double Straight.)

(21) KNOT (Main means the sea. The way to measure the 'rate' or speed at sea is with knots.)

19

LEVEL II

MORE ADVANCED
CRYPTIC CROSSWORDS

Providing you are still with me, and have not been taken to a place where sharp writing implements are not allowed, congratulations.

I cannot know the percentage of correct clues you achieved before resorting to the answers, but Level I was not easy for those new to Cryptics. If you thought so then you are already a competent Cryptic Crossword solver.

If you achieved less than fifty percent, I hope you read and re-read the answers until you understood how they were arrived at. More than fifty percent means you are using your mind with a newly acquired sense of reasoning, logic and word association; basically "thinking Cryptic".

There is a great deal of pride, sense of achievement and pleasure to be derived from the skill of understanding Cryptic Crosswords, not to mention the respect and admiration one gains from friends and colleagues. But take care not to appear a 'clever dick'.

If you find the remaining crosswords difficult, don't become despondent. You are very new to cryptics and the standard required to solve them usually takes years and many many crosswords to achieve. The important thing is to understand how the answers were arrived at. This is the purpose of the additional notes of explanation, which, from here on will be reduced in length. Comments will only be made where necessary. The level of difficulty will increase as we progress.

No. 1

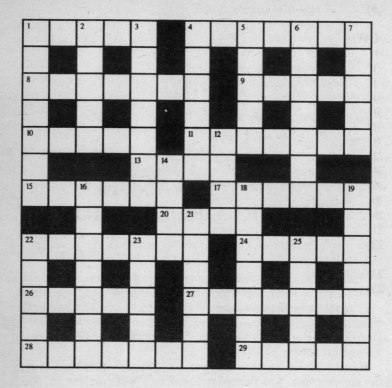

ACROSS

(1)   Coaches in Detroit Rams. (5)
(4)   Contract given to fliers. (7)
(8)   On another planet. (7)
(9)   Obviously unattractive. (5)
(10)   Tell to tidy up. (5)
(11)   Sounds like he's abroad keeping an eye on things. (7)
(13)   It could blow again. (4)
(15)   Areas for a W.C. (6)
(17)   Gently heat stew. (6)
(20)   The last word in a team entry. (4)
(22)   Shows place to operate. (7)
(24)   Animals need label in ship. (5)
(26)   Right in hock for a decapod. (5)
(27)   It's a sin to be greedy. (7)

(28) Russian got up to present a flower...... (3,4)
(29) ......English Midlands flower. (5)

DOWN

(1) The hour to leave to go on holiday. (4,3)
(2) Voiced opinion outside? (5)
(3) Moved around making trouble. (7)
(4) It's a grand place. (6)
(5) Take one a day to stay healthy. (5)
(6) Bar under the top light. (7)
(7) It's a washout. (5)
(12) Mad save to get the pot. (4)
(14) The Emperor was a sort of star. (4)
(16) The mere lad turned over a stone. (7)
(18) Precooked immediately. (7)
(19) Should give it to the elders. (7)
(21) Males one regards as a threat. (6)
(22) Thank the salesman for coming up to reduce the trousers. (5)
(23) Lawman's brave assistant? (5)
(25) An either / or requirement on a wanted poster. (5)

Answers to Crossword No. 1

ACROSS

(1)   TRAMS (Word From Two Words.)

(4)   CHARTER (As in 'Charter flight'.)

(8)   MARTIAN (Clue deliberately brief.)

(9)   PLAIN (Double Straight.)

(10)   ORDER (Double Straight.)

(11)   OVERSEE (Sounds Like: "Oversea".)

(13)   ETNA (Single Cryptic.)

(15)   FIELDS (Areas / W.C. Fields.)

(17)   SIMMER (Straight clue: gently heat; someone who is in a stew could be said to be simmering.)

(20)   AMEN (Word From Two Words.)

(22)   THEATRE (A shows place, and a place to operate is a theatre.)

(24)   STAGS (Label = TAG; 'in' ship = SS.)

(26)   PRAWN (Right = R; 'in' hock = PAWN; a prawn is a decapod.)

(27)   AVARICE (One of the seven deadly sins.)

(28)   RED ROSE (Too straightforward to explain.)

(29)   TRENT (Double Meaning: flow-er, not flower.)

DOWN

(1)   TIME OFF (Double Straight.)

(2)   AIRED (As in airing one's views.)

(3)   STIRRED (Double Straight clue.)

(4)   CANYON (Double Meaning.)

(5)   APPLE (As in "to keep the Doctor away.")

(6)   TRANSOM (A Transom is the horizontal bar under the fanlight, and over the main sash on a window or door.)

(7)   RINSE (Double Meaning clue.)

(12)   VASE (Anagram.)

(14)   TSAR (Anagram.)

(16)   EMERALD (Anagram.)

(18)   INSTANT (Double Straight: precooked as in mash or coffee, immediately is instant.)

(19)   RESPECT (Single Cryptic.)

(21)   MENACE (Males = MEN; one = ACE.)

(22)   TAPER (Thanks = TA; Salesman = REP; coming up = PER.)

(23)   TONTO (Double Meaning Word 'brave'.)

(25)   ALIVE (As in dead or alive.)

No. 2

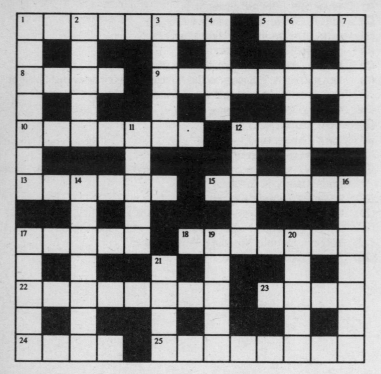

ACROSS

(1)   Could be a fair description of a vessel.... (4,4)
(5)   ....or the sack. (1,3)
(8)   Choose not to eat properly. (4)
(9)   Attempt to follow records of 1066. (8)
(10)   A five to one rota is taken back to pilot. (7)
(12)   Short note about fire. (5)
(13)   Illusions of goals. (6)
(15)   Park for 10. (6)
(17)   Initially the Liverpool Union Railway needs identification,
       that's appalling. (5)
(18)   Folded credit gradually. (7)
(22)   Shorten the area of mooring place. (8)
(23)   Stagger to the dance. (4)
(24)   The Peer holds the sword. (4)
(25)   Edward held Red's money and was worried. (8)

DOWN

(1) Once around the ground for country. (7)
(2) The first two kids go below old theatre to get girl. (5)
(3) Do better at an alfresco party. (5)
(4) Measure square copy. (4)
(6) Slips over at the races. (7)
(7) Final reckoning time. (3,2)
(11) Shy Timothy got one penny. (5)
(12) Two run to Bridgehead. (5)
(14) A race he made gave pain. (7)
(16) Filled with holes he joked. (7)
(17) Stick in the house. (5)
(19) Now time in Rio can be entertaining. (5)
(20) Hard crime to say. (5)
(21) Note that the picture is sharp. (4)

Answers to Crossword No. 2

ACROSS

(1)   LOVE BOAT (Double Meaning Word 'fair'.)

(5)   A BED (Continuation dots associate 'fair description', a description of a bed could be 'the sack'. As in 'hitting the sack'.)

(8)   PICK (Double Straight.)

(9)   TAPESTRY (Attempt = TRY, to follow records = TAPES.)

(10)   AVIATOR (Whole Word: A; five = V, to I; rota taken back = ATOR.)

(12)   BRIEF (Note = B; anagram of fire = RIEF.)

(13)   DREAMS (Double Straight.)

(15)   HANGAR (The 10, in this instance, indicates the clue number 10, not an X. An aviator parks up in a hangar.)

(17)   LURID (Initials LUR; identification = ID.)

(18)   CREASED (Credit = CR; gradually = EASED.)

(22)   DOCKLAND (Shorten = DOCK; area = LAND.)

(23)   REEL (Double Straight.)

(24)   EPEE (ThE PEEr.)

(25)   TROUBLED (Edward = T......ED; Red money = ROUBLE.)

DOWN

(1) LAPLAND (Once around = LAP; ground = LAND.)

(2) VICKI (First two KIds; old theatre = VIC, as in the 'Old Vic'.)

(3) OUTDO (Alfresco = OUT; party = DO.)

(4) TAPE (Square = T; copy = APE.)

(6) BETTING (An interesting clue. Double Meaning: 'slips'; over meaning 'over there', not a tumble.)

(7) DAY OF (As in the day of reckoning.)

(11) TIMID (Timothy = TIM; I; penny = D.)

(12) BRACE (Run = RACE; Bridge'head' = B; a BRACE is a pair or two of something.)

(14) EARACHE (Anagram.)

(16) RIDDLED (Double Straight.)

(17) LODGE (Double Straight.)

(19) RADIO (Now time = AD; 'in' R--IO.)

(20) STEEL (Crime = steal.)

(21) DART (Note = D; picture = ART.)

No. 3

ACROSS

(7)   Members of CID show for certain, innocent. (8)
(8)   Father came back after him for lots of money. (4)
(9)   Do away with inside Secret Service, there's talent. (6)
(10) Give mischief maker drawings. (6)
(11) Cain changed ancient Peruvian. (4)
(12) Travelling in car to junction in the dock. (8)
(14) Relied upon the section being finished. (8)
(18) Stare at Lego set. (4)
(20) It forms a division in the church. (6)
(22) Take off separates. (6)
(23) Give up part of the nice deal. (4)
(24) Get accustomed to the nearest pub. (8)

DOWN

(1) Go down. (6)
(2) Remains of the turnover. (8)
(3) How to play dead good. (6)
(4) Only half a way to clear a window. (6)
(5) Stow away vessel. (4)
(6) Sounds rich but far from it. (6)
(13) When the last one goes down it's a topping time. (4,4)
(15) Pass once and make note of the flower coming up. (6)
(16) Limped away with only a small dent. (6)
(17) Holmes always did it. (6)
(19) Failed to get copper for winged insect. (6)
(21) I am cross, in fact I've really got the goat. (4)

Answers to Crossword No. 3

ACROSS

(7) DISPROVE (CID = DIS; for certain = PROVE.)

(8) HEAP (Father = PA; come back = AP; 'after' him = HE-AP.)

(9) SKILLS (Do away with = KILL; inside S....S.)

(10) IMPART (Mischief maker = IMP; drawings = ART.)

(11) INCA (Anagram of CAIN.)

(12) MOTORING (Junction = T; dock = MO-ORING.)

(14) DEPENDED (Section = DEPartment; finished = ENDED.)

(18) OGLE (Anagram of LEGO.)

(20) SCHISM (Double Meaning Word 'division'. An uncommon word meaning a separating of a church into two as a result of division of opinion.)

(22) DETACH (Double Straight.)

(23) CEDE (niCE DEal.)

(24) LOCALISE (Single Cryptic.)

DOWN
(1) SICKEN (Double Meaning Word 'down'.)
(2) SPILLAGE (Single Cryptic.)
(3) POSSUM (A possum, as part of its defence, plays dead.)
(4) DEMIST (Half = DEMI; a way = ST.)
(5) SHIP (Double Straight: to 'ship' is to pack.)
(6) BARREN (Sounds Like baron.)
(13) ROOF TILE (When roofers finish a roof, they celebrate with a 'topping out ceremony'.)
(15) EXCEED (Once = EX; note = C; flower = DEE.)
(16) DIMPLE (Anagram of LIMPED.)
(17) DEDUCE (Single Cryptic.)
(19) LOCUST (Failed = LO..ST; 'to get' indicates an Inside clue; insert copper = CU.)
(21) IBEX (I am = I BE; cross = X.)

No. 4

ACROSS

(1) High up in the local often. (5)
(4) Facial expression as a result of chewing limes. (5)
(9) Small charts for the horses. (7)
(10) Anaesthetic given nearby. (5)
(11) Cheat took off building material for Island. (5)
(12) It's free to enter five points for flavouring. (7)
(14) A small bit of litter. (4)
(16) Approve note reduction. (5)
(18) Stare wildly at a bloom. (5)
(21) Make money in Tyne and Wear North. (4)
(24) Film direction? (7)
(26) Animal that must be removed from a hot terrain. (5)
(28) Throw out the alien going round the old theatre. (5)

(29) Granted one's well off. (7)
(30) Wide mouthed after a parting note. (5)
(31) A row of sleepers. (5)

DOWN

(2) Remain having time off. (5)
(3) Strainers for photographers. (7)
(5) Unusual Salem people. (5)
(6) It's given to poet for total freedom. (7)
(7) A southern writer in Colorado. (5)
(8) Put short distance around General and be quick. (5)
(9) Bag for the boot. (4)
(13) Bill header. (4)
(15) Person to take advantage of a Junkie. (4)
(17) Tail ender mixed drink for ages. (7)
(19) Lord of the mountain? (7)
(20) Last ones to cry over a puppet. (5)
(22) Converting ragen is making me mad. (5)
(23) Dart up to see Jazz. (4)
(25) Finish high tea. (3,2)
(27) He pulls bridge. (5)

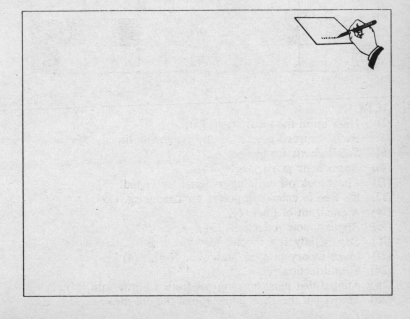

Answers to Crossword No. 4

ACROSS

(1)   ALOFT (LoCAL OFTen.)

(4)   SMILE (Anagram of limes.)

(9)   STABLES (Small = S; charts = TABLES.)

(10) LOCAL (Double Straight.)

(11) CRETE (Cheat = con taken off conCRETE.)

(12) ESSENCE (Free = NC, entering five points ESSEncE.)

(14) RUNT (Double Meaning 'litter': the runt of a litter is the smallest one, or one that doesn't come up to size.)

(16) BLESS (Note = B; reduction = LESS.)

(18) ASTER (Anagram of 'stare'.)

(21) EARN (WEAR North.)

(24) WESTERN (Double Straight.)

(26) OTTER (hOT TERrain.)

(28) EVICT (Alien = ET going round VIC.)

(29) ENDOWED (Double Straight.)

(30) AGAPE (A; parting = GAP; note = E.)

(31) SNORE (Double Meaning 'row'.)

DOWN

(2)   LEAVE (Double Straight.)

(3)   FILTERS (Double Straight: lens filters form an essential part of a photographer's equipment.)

(5)   MALES (Anagram of Salem.)

(6)   LICENCE (As in poetic licence.)

(7)   ASPEN (A southern = AS; writer = PEN.)

(8)   FLEET (Short distance = F...T, General = LEE.)

(9)   SACK (Double Straight: the word 'boot' is slang for getting the sack.)

(13) STAR (Double Meaning 'bill'.)

(15) USER (Double Straight.)

(17) LASTING (Tail ender = LAST; mixed, meaning an anagram of a drink = gin = ING.)

(19) SNOWDON (Single Cryptic: Mt. Snowdon, Lord Snowdon.)

(20) SWEEP (Last oneS; cry = WEEP.)

(22) ANGER (Anagram of 'ragen'.)

(23) TRAD (Up = write the word 'dart' upwards from the bottom of the grid.)

(25) EAT UP (Single Cryptic: 'up' = high.)

(27) TOWER (Double Straight.)

No. 5

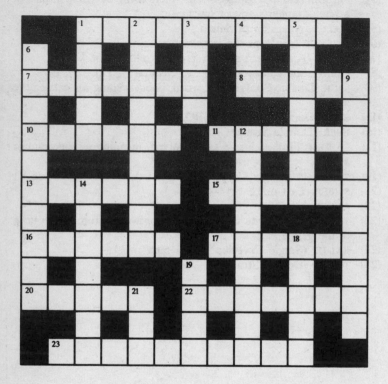

ACROSS

(1)　One carpet I add on to move. (10)
(7)　Impression that I am going to get published. (7)
(8)　Soldier got into cover for a spell. (5)
(10)　Takes all the profit from the dairy. (6)
(11)　Short periodical to mineworkers' union (could be fired). (6)
(13)　Minor insult. (6)
(15)　A father to a rebel was a brave man. (6)
(16)　Attack Dave in madness. (6)
(17)　Skirt around. (6)
(20)　How one can get material from two small capitals. (5)
(22)　That's a nice way to bring the kids up. (7)
(23)　Direction from cookery teacher regarding following term. (4,6)

DOWN

(1)   A representative the French had enough of. (5)
(2)   Motorcycle Ted won on? (9)
(3)   Half a farthing for the little one. (4)
(4)   This man repeatedly would get a drum. (3)
(5)   It is natural to go in car to organize. (7)
(6)   Talk about a meeting. (10)
(9)   Ability to enter a race for nothing and got a point. (10)
(12) A bubble bath darling, come up and get something to eat. (9)
(14) Don't exclude affect. (7)
(18) Lenin once held fine material. (5)
(19) Give away church to the Department of the Environment. (4)
(21) Ten lifted the mesh. (3)

Answers to Crossword No. 5
ACROSS
(1)   AUTOMATION (One = AUTO; carpet = MAT; I; add ON.)
(7)   IMPRINT (I am = I'M; published = PRINT.)
(8)   MAGIC (Soldier = GI; cover = MA..C.)
(10)   CREAMS (Double Straight.)
(11)   MAGNUM (Short periodical = MAG-azine; mineworkers' union
       = N.U.M.; a magnum is a gun that could be fired.)
(13)   SLIGHT (Double Straight.)
(15)   APACHE (A father = A PA; rebel = CHE Guevara.)
(16)   INVADE (Anagram of DAVE IN.)
(17)   FRINGE (Double Straight.)
(20)   NYLON (Two 'small' capitals = NY and LON.)
(22)   EUGENIC (Single Cryptic. Were it not for the fact that the word
       is uncommon, it would be a Straight clue.)
(23)   NEXT SEASON (Cryptic first, Straight last.)

DOWN

(1) AMPLE (A representative = A MP; the French = LE.)

(2) TRIUMPHED (Motorcycle = TRIUMPH; Ted = ED.)

(3) MITE (Half a farthing is a MITE.)

(4) TOM (Half of a TOM tom.)

(5) ORGANIC (Anagram of GO IN CAR.)

(6) DISCUSSION (Double Straight.)

(9) COMPETENCE (Enter a race = COMPETE; for nothing = no charge = NC; a point = E.)

(12) ASPARAGUS (A; bubble bath = SPA; darling = SUGAR, come up = reverse sugar = RAGUS.)

(14) INVOLVE (Double Straight.)

(18) NINON (LeNIN ONce. Ninon is a finely woven material.)

(19) CEDE (Church = C of E, Dep of Env.)

(21) NET (Ten lifted = NET.)

No. 6

ACROSS

(7) Hit a six and four to the wood strip. (6)
(8) It's said the country home has style. (6)
(9) Hurry for support. (4)
(10) Charm your way in. (8)
(11) Packed up walking. (6)
(13) Inside, now it hindered. (6)
(14) Announce the Newspaper's name. (6)
(16) A leach will do it to clean. (6)
(18) Quick way on M25. (4,4)
(20) David lost five hundred but still keen. (4)
(22) Lose in court brief, ended up in small room. (6)
(23) Lorraine showed the way and lounged around. (6)

DOWN
- (1) It's the end of the game pal. (4)
- (2) Tasted awful it's said. (6)
- (3) Meant to see fiancé. (8)
- (4) Must change I'm dirty. (4)
- (5) Young fashionable supporter goes down to square. (6)
- (6) Change it round the doctrine. (8)
- (12) Last word can be acceptable. (8)
- (13) Direction too soon we hear where the wind's coming from. (8)
- (15) Witness warrant. (6)
- (17) Medium sort of consultant. (6)
- (19) Bill's pretending. (4)
- (21) Type of butter? (4)

Answers to Crossword No. 6

ACROSS

(7)   BATTEN (Hit = BAT; six & four = TEN.)

(8)   MANNER (Sounds Like manor.)

(9)   BELT (Double Straight.)

(10) ENTRANCE (Double Straight: entrance as in 'way in', entrance as in to 'captivate'.)

(11) PADDED (Packed as in 'enlarged' or 'padded out'; slow walk.)

(13) WITHIN (Now IT HINdered.)

(14) HERALD (Double Straight.)

(16) SPONGE (Double Straight.)

(18) FAST LANE (Double Straight.)

(20) AVID ('Lost five hundred' means to remove a 'D' from dAVID.)

(22) CLOSET (LOSE inside abbreviation of court = CT.)

(23) LOLLED (Abbreviation of Lorraine = LOL; showed the way = LED.)

DOWN

(1) MATE (Single Cryptic.)

(2) STATED (Anagram of TASTED.)

(3) INTENDED (Double Straight.)

(4) SMUT (Anagram of MUST.)

(5) INFANT (Fashionable = IN; supporter = FAN; square = T.)

(6) TEACHING (Anagram of CHANGE IT.)

(12) AMENABLE (Last word = AMEN; can = ABLE.)

(13) WESTERLY (Direction = WEST; 'too soon' Sounds Like early = ERLY.)

(15) ATTEST (Double Straight.)

(17) ORACLE (Double Meaning of 'medium'.)

(19) ACTS (Double Straight.)

(21) IBEX (Butter = goat.)

No. 7

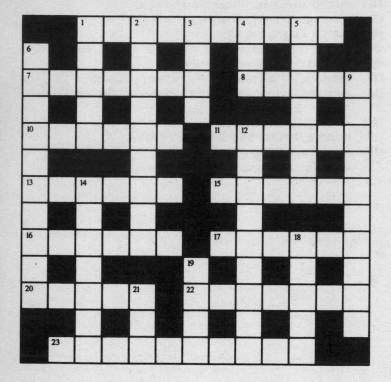

ACROSS

(1) Early nursing act. (10)

(7) Square up with money is a nuisance. (7)

(8) Substance contained by some talented people. (5)

(10) Gasp at the bra change. (6)

(11) Give a last face lift? (6)

(13) Grades to see what's true. (6)

(15) Disorganised way we changed in the navy. (6)

(16) Good man will travel by foot. (6)

(17) I hear the fortune teller made money. (6)

(20) Alex Haley's background? (5)

(22) Blimey, nothing so complete as a bottle of wine. (7)

(23) Arnold's the man to end it. (10)

DOWN

(1)   Quiet girl gives written language. (5)
(2)   I turned and fought being in combat. (9)
(3)   Either way she went north for revenge. (4)
(4)   Reduce a short measure. (3)
(5)   I say there is lateshift allowance to boost the plant. (7)
(6)   A resistor of rock and roll. (10)
(9)   Fixed nail to main layer. (10)
(12) Travel test for car or ship for speeding in the main. (9)
(14) Talkative Bo veers away. (7)
(18) Taken to dance. (5)
(19) Heir has nothing shortly. (4)
(21) Some say it's the end. (3)

Answers to Crossword No. 7
ACROSS
(1)   PRETENDING (Early = PRE; nursing = TENDING; to act is to pretend.)
(7)   TROUBLE (Square = T; money = ROUBLE.)
(8)   METAL (SOME TALented.)
(10)   BREATH (Anagram of THE BRA.)
(11)   EMBALM (Single Cryptic.)
(13)   LEVELS (Double Straight: to judge 'trueness' one uses a spirit level.)
(15)   STREWN (Way = ST; we changed = EW; in the R..N.)
(16)   STRIDE (Good man = ST; travel = RIDE.)
(17)   PROFIT (Sounds Like a prophet.)
(20)   ROOTS (Alex Haley wrote 'Roots'.)
(22)   OLOROSO (Blimey = O'LOR; nothing = O; SO whole word.)
(23)   TERMINATOR (Double Straight'ish'.)

DOWN

(1)   PROSE (Quiet = P; girl = ROSE.)

(2)   EMBATTLED (I = me, turned = EM; fought = BATTLED.)

(3)   EVEN (Either way she = EVE (reversible); north = N.)

(4)   DIM (Short DIMension.)

(5)   NITRATE (Sounds Like night rate.)

(6)   STABILISER (Single Cryptic.) Nice clue, this is what cryptics
       are about.

(9)   LAMINATION (Anagram of NAIL TO MAIN.)

(12)   MOTORBOAT (Test for car = MOT; OR; ship = BOAT.)

(14)   VERBOSE (Anagram of BO VEERS.)

(18)   FLOOR (Single Cryptic. One takes to the floor when
       dancing.)

(19)   SOON (Heir = SON; has nothing = O.)

(21)   SUM (Sounds Like some; the end total.)

No. 8

ACROSS

(6) Indicate that Ed changed a fiver. (6)

(7) A hundred go halve. (6)

(8) Royal document sent into the Lords regarding entertainers. (10)

(10) Din ref made for mate. (6)

(11) Up the creek looking for timber. (6)

(12) Boxer tore into chief Commanding Officer over material. (6)

(15) They often come second. (6)

(17) Raids the store before the bad weather. (10)

(18) No rubbish. (6)

(19) Injuries from dancing? (6)

DOWN
(1) Fence distributor. (6)
(2) Close finish. (10)
(3) Communist followed fighter and gave dirty looks. (6)
(4) Train several classes. (6)
(5) Not keen on the rhyme. (6)
(9) Arm vessel to join club...... (10)
(13) ....and went back to a club to approach newspaperman. (6)
(14) Confusion re lost horseman. (6)
(15) Odds on a celebration for Puck. (6)
(16) Lift glass to free stoats. (6)

Answers to Crossword No. 8
ACROSS
(6)   DENOTE (Ed changed = DE: fiver = NOTE.)
(7)   CLEAVE (Hundred = C; go = LEAVE.)
(8)   PERFORMERS (Royal = R; document = FORM; into lords = PE.....ERS.)
(10)   FRIEND (Anagram of DIN REF.)
(11)   LUMBER (To be up the creek could be to be in lumber.)
(12)   CALICO (Boxer = ALI; chief commanding officer = C...CO.)
(15)   SWEETS (Second, as in seconds or pudding.)
(17)   BARNSTORMS (Store = BARN; bad weather = STORMS.)
(18)   REFUSE (Say no is to REFUSE; rubbish is REFUSE.)
(19)   TWISTS (Single Cryptic.)

DOWN
(1) DEALER (Double Straight.)
(2) COMPLETION (Double Straight.)
(3) LEERED (Fighter = Bruce LEE, communist = RED.)
(4) SCHOOL (Double Straight.)
(5) AVERSE (Whole Word A; rhyme = VERSE.)
(9) MEMBERSHIP (Arm = MEMBER; vessel = SHIP.)
(13) ABATED (Continuation dots associate 'clubs': Whole Word (letter) A; club = BAT; newspaperman = ED.)
(14) OSTLER (Anagram of RE LOST.)
(15) SPRITE (Odds = SP; celebration = RITE.)
(16) TOASTS (Anagram of STOATS.)

No. 9

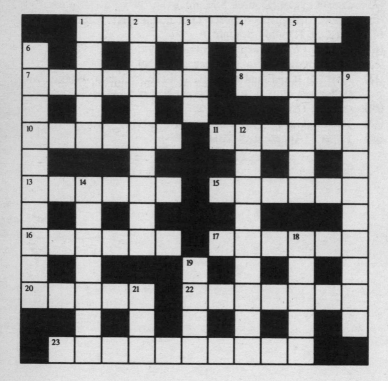

ACROSS

(1)   Calm loch has comforting qualities. (10)

(7)   Catch the girl said the man without any thought for others. (7)

(8)   Cooking broth is such a pain. (5)

(10)   It's mainly used for steering. (6)

(11)   The Yank says the girl needs mineral and lots of it. (6)

(13)   Opened the door to the newsman. (6)

(15)   A view from a spectacular place. (6)

(16)   Remake it dear, and give them a mouthful. (6)

(17)   You and I like the Spaniard but he's an animal. (6)

(20)   Doctor (First) went on and on and on. (5)

(22)   They come good at Christmas. (7)

(23)   No more star treatment for him. (10)

DOWN

(1) A super amount of money. (5)
(2) What a wonderful thing the lord did. (5,4)
(3) This is the twelfth letter to the animal transporter, what a caper. (4)
(4) Lift a weight, or can't. (3)
(5) He changed his mind about Christmas. (7)
(6) Caused trouble and reawakened an old injury. (10)
(9) Inhale at a lower rate will leave one so. (10)
(12) Dam stream circling place in Holland. (9)
(14) A complaint to worry about. (7)
(18) A deep sounding noise. (5)
(19) It was a real shock being endlessly stung. (4)
(21) Stray from the centre of Derry. (3)

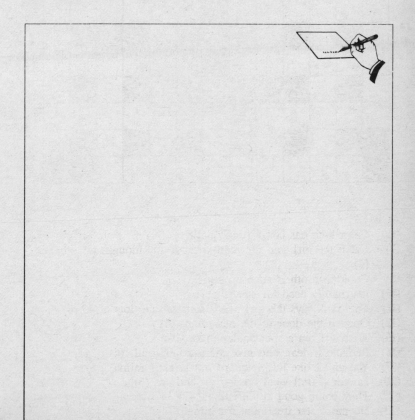

Answers to Crossword No. 9

ACROSS

(1) GENTLENESS (Calm = GENTLE; loch = NESS.)

(7) GRABBER (Sounds Like 'grab her'.)

(8) THROB (Anagram of BROTH.)

(10) RUDDER ('Mainly' means pertaining to the sea.)

(11) GALORE (Yank says girl = GAL; mineral = ORE.)

(13) VENTED (Door = VENT; newsman = ED.)

(15) ASPECT (A SPECTacular.)

(16) TIRADE (Anagram of IT DEAR.)

(17) WEASEL (You and I = WE; like = AS; the Spaniard = EL.)

(20) DRONE (Doctor = DR; first = ONE.)

(22) TIDINGS (Single Cryptic.)

(23) ASTRONOMER (Anagram of NO MORE STAR.)

DOWN

(1)   GRAND (Single Cryptic.)

(2)   NOBLE DEED (Lord = NOBLE; did = DEED.)

(3)   LARK (Twelfth letter = L; animal transporter = ARK; caper = LARK.)

(4)   NOT (Lift indicates reversing letters.)

(5)   SCROOGE (His mind was changed by the visitations of the ghosts.)

(6)   AGGRAVATED (Double Straight.)

(9)   BREATHLESS (Inhale = BREATH; lower rate = LESS.)

(12)   AMSTERDAM (Anagram of DAM STREAM.)

(14)   NERVOUS (Double Straight.)

(18)   SONAR (Double Meaning: 'DEEP'.)

(19)   STUN (Endless STUN-G.)

(21)   ERR (dERRy.)

No. 10

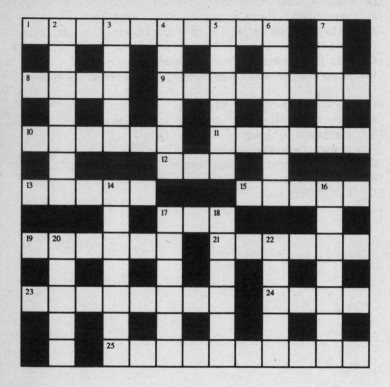

ACROSS

(1)   Sign up for full time service. (4,3,3)
(8)   Fuel points? (4)
(9)   Fought for disposal. (8)
(10)   A difference between Lance and squaddie. (6)
(11)   Fools do it is barmy. (6)
(12)   Manage to tick over. (3)
(13)   Load of money for jam. (5)
(15)   Place for a good deal of selling. (1,4)
(17)   Last words of freedom? (1,2)
(19)   Ivy's first name was taken by Juliet. (6)
(21)   Clock service....(6)
(23)   ....stops here. (8)
(24)   See 2 Down.
(25)   Organize match. (2-8)

DOWN

(2 & 24 Across) Give me the money and I'll blame someone else. (4,3,4)

(3) I moan about her. (5)

(4) Well known name to backer. (6)

(5) He made a monkey out of everyone. (6)

(6) Yes food for the rich kids. (7)

(7) A hundred take it easy at the top. (5)

(14) It's in the belly. (7)

(16) Incline to slice meat for Mr. Spratt. (4,3)

(17) Go in Di mix a colour. (6)

(18) Insult after reaching the end of the plank? (6)

(20) Elated to be on the radio. (2,3)

(22) Place for driver in home. (5)

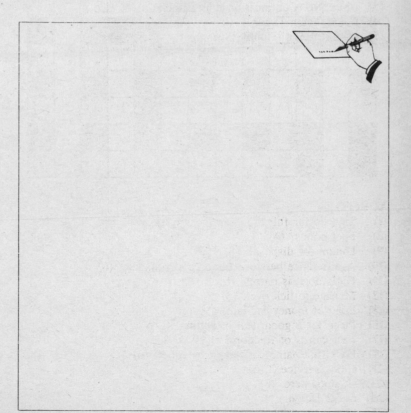

Answers to Crossword No. 10
ACROSS
(1)   OPEN ALL DAY (Double Meaning: 'sign up'.)
(8)   ESSO (Abbreviations.)
(9)   SCRAPPED (Double Straight.)
(10) STRIPE (Single Cryptic: Lance Corporal and ordinary soldier.)
(11) IDIOTS (Anagram of DO IT IS.)
(12) RUN (Double Straight.)
(13) WEDGE (Double Straight: wedge of money, get wedged in.)
(15) A SALE (Double Meaning: 'good deal'.)
(17) I DO (This will upset a few, but it's a crossword clue not my personal opinion.)
(19) POISON (Double Straight.)
(21) FACIAL (Clock as in cockney for 'face'.)
(23) HAIRLINE (Continuation dots association is face.)
(24) BUCK (See 2 Down.)
(25) CO-ORDINATE (Double Straight.)

DOWN

(2) PASS THE (Double Straight.)

(3) NAOMI (Anagram of I MOAN.)

(4) LESTER (Cryptic: backers or gamblers know LESTER Piggott.)

(5) DARWIN (Single Cryptic. It refers to Charles Darwin's book *The Origin of the Species*, where he formed the theory that mankind originated from apes.)

(6) YUPPIES (Yes = YUP; food = PIES.)

(7) CREST (Hundred = C; take it easy = REST.)

(14) GASTRIC (Single Cryptic.)

(16) LEAN CUT (Incline = LEAN; slice meat = CUT.)

(17) INDIGO (Anagram of GO IN DI.)

(18) OFFEND (OFF-END.)

(20) ON AIR (Double Straight.)

(22) CABIN (Double Straight.)

No. 11

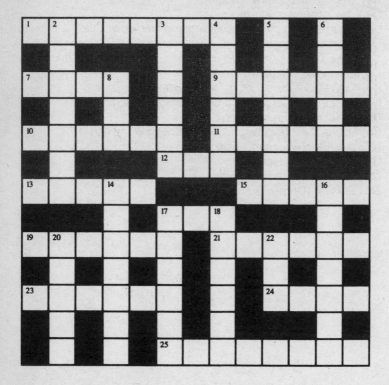

ACROSS

(1)   Thatcher's directive to laundry woman? (4,4)
(7)   Familiar with American newspaperman. (4)
(9)   Irony of a high lob. (6)
(10) Some people cherish a greedy dirty man. (6)
(11) The header taken star shook the Scots football team. (6)
(12) A system to compute. (3)
(13) Action to take to get a raise. (5)
(15) It's cast down before growing up. (1,4)
(17) Pictures from Cartier Bresson. (3)
(19) Represents at a match. (6)
(21) A loud showground business. (6)
(23) Top teacher's wish. (6)
(24) Catch on the pony's tail. (4)
(25) It's a good hand, honest. (8)

DOWN

(2)   With reference to admiration. (7)
(3)   A loud car to manage. (6)
(4)   Shy out playing with kids. (6)
(5)   Note you and I hand over for cheap travel. (3,4)
(6)   Cry after first son went on photographic trip. (5)
(8)   First on the scales. (3)
(14) Nail the top man down he's a fool. (7)
(16) Grave word indeed. (7)
(17) Remarks top teams make. (6)
(18) Sample square flower. (6)
(20) You'd put these into it in a problem. (5)
(22) Conform well. (3)

Answers to Crossword No. 11
ACROSS
(1)   IRON LADY (Single Cryptic.)

(7)   USED (American newspaperman = US ED.)

(9)   UPSHOT (Single Cryptic.)

(10)   LECHER (PeopLE CHERish.)

(11)   HEARTS (The header taken means remove the 'T' from 'the' leaving HE; Anagram of STAR.)

(12)   DOS (Dos is the most popular computer operating system.)

(13)   STEPS (Single Cryptic.)

(15)   A SEED (Single Cryptic.)

(17)   ART (CARTier.)

(19)   STANDS (Double Straight.)

(21)   AFFAIR (A loud = AF; showground = FAIR.)

(23)   BEHEAD (A teacher's wish is to BE HEAD.)

(24)   TRAP (Very cryptic: a trap goes on the pony's tail.)

(25)   STRAIGHT (Hand, as in poker.)

DOWN

(2)	RESPECT (Double Straight.)
(3)	AFFORD (A loud = AF; car = FORD.)
(4)	YOUTHS (Anagram of SHY OUT.)
(5)	BUS PASS (Note = B; you and I = US; hand over = PASS.)
(6)	SHOOT (A cry is a HOOT; first of son is S.)
(8)	DOH (As in doh-ray-me.)
(14)	PINHEAD (Nail = PIN; top man = HEAD.)
(16)	EPITAPH (Double Meaning Word: 'grave'.)
(17)	ASIDES (top teams = 'A' SIDES.)
(18)	TASTER (Square = T, flower = ASTER.)
(20)	TEETH (As in "get your teeth into it".)
(22)	FIT (Double Straight.)

No. 12

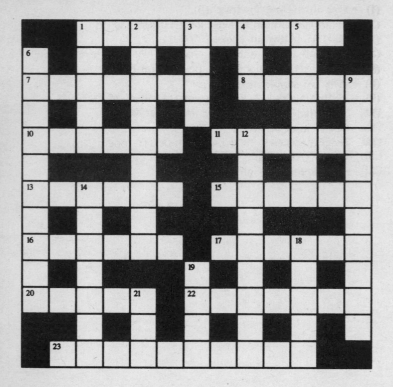

ACROSS

(1)   Appropriate description of something that could be put on. (10)

(7)   Really didn't like the red pole position. (7)

(8)   Lashes out just for fun. (5)

(10) A place where one must wear cool headwear. (3,3)

(11) Got H.R.N. together. (6)

(13) The little devil went outside to freshen up but it won't do him any good. (6)

(15) Turn up suddenly, waving a paper. (6)

(16) Edging forward to look around. (6)

(17) Flicks a mince pie. (6)

(20) Ascertain that fifty only do it for money. (5)

(22) Reveal death is not altogether final. (4,3)

(23) What one should eat to gain pounds. (10)

DOWN

(1) One in the eye for love. (5)

(2) Professional club has one on trial period. (9)

(3) One from Kuwait Emirate. (4)

(4) Vessel that first docked at Ararat. (3)

(5) Sent the bill in to forget about the milk. (7)

(6) A spare supplement. (10)

(9) He maintains he's just a sweet old man. (5,5)

(12) State that Miss Shapiro returned to. (9)

(14) After time for delivery. (7)

(18) Example is held in the Cathedral, of a poem. (5)

(19) I'm told it's very deep to be on my own. (4)

(21) Three points for getting there. (3)

Answers to Crossword No. 12

ACROSS

(1) APPLICABLE (Single Cryptic.)
(7) DEPLORE (Anagram of RED POLE.)
(8) KICKS (Double Straight.)
(10) ICE CAP (Single Cryptic.)
(11) THRONG (Anagram of GOT H.R.N.)
(13) IMPAIR (Little devil = IMP; freshen up outside = AIR.)
(15) APPEAR (Anagram of A PAPER.)
(16) NOSING (Double Cryptic.)
(17) CINEMA (Anagram of A MINCE; the 'flicks' are the pictures.)
(20) LEARN (Fifty = L; do it for money = EARN.)
(22) OPEN END (Reveal = OPEN; death = END.)
(23) GENEROUSLY (Single Cryptic.)

DOWN

(1) APPLE (As with 'apple of my eye'.)
(2) PROBATION (Professional = PRO; club = BAT; has I ON.)
(3) ITEM (KuwaIT EMirate.)
(4) ARK (The ark docked after the flood at Ararat.)
(5) LACTOSE (The bill = ACT; forget about = LOSE; milk
     contains lactose.)
(6) ADDITIONAL (Double Straight.)
(9) SUGAR DADDY (Double Cryptic.)
(12) HAPPINESS (As with Helen Shapiro's song *Walking Back to
     Happiness*.)
(14) POSTAGE (After = POST; time = AGE.)
(18) ELEGY (Example = EG, Cathedral = ELY.)
(19) SOLO (Sounds like 'so low'.)
(21) NEE (Getting there, meaning to be born.)

PART THREE
REFERENCE

20

WORD EXCHANGING LISTS

The following pages are lists of regularly used 'Word Exchanging' words, consisting of two to five letters. I have limited the number of letters, as opposed to giving all possibilities disregarding dimensions of words, for two reasons.

One, I could give many lists of names of famous painters, birds, types of rock, poets etc., but then the challenge of completing a crossword would become nothing more than a lengthy process of mere reference. Hardly mind expanding, not to mention the fact that it would necessitate a significantly larger book than a dictionary. Secondly, the objective is not to supply the 'straight' answer to a clue, but to give assistance with the sections that make up the word/answer required. This is far more important, as it will lead you to an understanding of crypticism.

Although the list is fairly long, all the selected words are commonplace in cryptic crosswords.

A

Able .... CAN
Above .... OVER
Agent .... SPY or REP
Allow .... LET
Also .... AND
Anger .... RAGE or IRE
Auto .... CAR

B

Ban .... BAR
Bar .... BAN
Beer .... ALE
Behold .... LO
Belt .... HIT
Block .... DAM
Bridge .... CROSS or SPAN
Business .... FIRM

C

Can .... ABLE or TIN
Card .... ACE
Chop .... AXE
Clock .... TIMER
Communist .... RED
Company .... FIRM
Copy .... APE
Crazy .... MAD
Crime .... SIN

D

Dance .... REEL
Dead .... LATE
Denial .... NO
Deserve .... EARN
Devil .... IMP
Discard .... SHED

Disturbance .... ROW
Dodge .... MISS
Dog .... CUR
Downpour .... RAIN
Duty .... TOLL or TAX
Dynasty .... MING

E

Each .... ALL
Eaten .... ATE
Elapse .... PASS
Elevator .... LIFT
Eleven .... SIDE
Employ .... USE
Encore .... MORE
End .... LAST
Entire .... ALL
Every .... EACH
Ex .... WAS
Exam .... TEST
Expensive .... DEAR

F

Falsehood .... LIE
Fashionable .... IN
Father .... DAD or PA
Feed .... EAT
Fib .... LIE
Field .... LEA
Fight .... SPAR
Fire .... AXE
First man .... ADAM
First woman .... EVE
Fish ..... LING, COD, DAB etc
Fix .... MEND
Flat .... EVEN or PAD
Flatten .... IRON
Flower .... NILE, DEE, etc
Flower ..... ASTER, ROSE etc

G

Gamble .... BET
Gammon .... HAM
Gang .... MOB
Gate .... DOOR
General .... LEE, IKE
Germ .... BUG
Girl .... HER, SHE, LASS
Gloomy .... SAD
Goal .... AIM
God .... LORD
Gossip .... CHAT
Gun .. GAT, BREN, STEN or ARM
Guided .... LED

H

Harness .... TIE
Hat .... CAP
Have .... OWN
Hence .... SO
Heir .... SON
Her .... SHE
Hill .... TOR
Hound .... DOG

I

I .... ME
Idea .... PLAN
Identical .... SAME
Ignore .... OMIT
Ill .... BAD
Illustrate .... DRAW
Imitate .... APE
Inactive .... IDLE
Individual .... ONE
Inert .... DEAD
Inn .... PUB
Irate .... MAD
Ivy .... VINE

J

Jack .... SALT, TAR
Jar .... URN
Jug .... EWER
Just .... FAIR
Juvenile .... KID

K

Keep .... HOLD
Khan .... AGA
Kill .... SLAY
Knot .... TIE, REEF

L

Lair .... DEN
Last .... END
Late .... DEAD
Layer .... HEN
Lease .... HIRE, RENT
Leather .... HIDE, SKIN
Level .... EVEN
Levy .... TAX
Like .... SAME
Livid .... MAD
Local ...... INN, NEAR, PUB
Lone .... ONE
Looker .... EYE
Lord .... GOD or PEER

M

Main .... SEA
Man . (Male Name) HE or HIM
Mark .... SCAR
Marry .... WED
Member ...... LEG or ARM
Mob .... GANG
Mother .... MA

N

Nail .... PIN
Nasty .... BAD
Near .... BY

Neckwear .... TIE
Needy .... POOR
Neon .... GAS
Nest .... HOME
Noise .... ROW
Nothing .... NIL
Notice .... BILL, SEE

O

Observe .... SEE
Obstruct .... BAR
Old .... AGE
Omega .... END
On Board .... SHIP
Opening .... DOOR
Orderly .... NEAT
Orient .... EAST
Overcome .... BEAT
Owns .... HAS

P

Paddle .... OAR
Particle .... ION
Party .... DO
Party ...... LIB, LAB or CON
Passed .... DIE
Payment .... FEE
Peer .... LORD
Plead .... BEG
Port .... WINE, LEFT
Pose .... SIT
Possess .... OWN
Proceed .... GO
Pub .... INN

Q

Quantity .... SOME
Quarrel .... ROW
Quit .... GO
Quixote .... DON

R

Rage .... IRE
Rail .... LINE
Rasputin .... MONK
Record .... DISC
Refusal .... NO
Regulation .... LAW
Remedy .... CURE
Rodent .... RAT
Route .... WAY
Runner .... BOSS, SKI

S

Sailor ...... HAND, JACK, TAR
Scar .... MARK
School .... ETON
Sea .... MAIN
She .... HER
Sit .... POSE
Small drink ...... NIP or TOT
Smallholding .... PLOT
Smooth .... FLAT or EVEN
Son .... HEIR
Speed .... RATE
Star .... SUN
Study .... DEN
Stumble .... TRIP or FALL
Sum .... ADD
Swimmer .... EEL

T

Taxi .... CAB
Team .... SIDE
Tether .... TIE
Thanks .... TA
The French .... LE or LA

Time .... AGE
Title .... NAME
Tune .... AIR

U

Under .... SUB
Unhealthy .... BAD, ILL
Unit .... ONE

V

Vehicle .... CAR
Victory .... WIN

W

Wage .... PAY
Wager .... BET
Watch .... TIMER or EYE
Wizard .... OZ
Woman .... HER or SHE
Worker ... HAND, ANT or BEE
Writer .... PEN

Y

Yale .... LOCK
Yarn .... LIE
Yearn .... YEN
You and I .... WE or US
Young fish .... FRY
Youth .... LAD

Z

Zany .... MAD
Zest .... GO
Zeus .... GOD
Zip .... FLY

21

CROSSWORDS IN NEWSPAPERS

Whether or not it is a newspaper of your particular political persuasion or taste, *The Sun* has a good cryptic crossword for beginners. It has a set of Straight clues as well as Cryptic, which require the same answers. This of course assists in indicating the 'straight' section of a clue to cross refer. E.g.

Cryptic — (2) Ground and ground letters. (9)

Straight — (2) Innkeepers. (9)

It's pretty obvious now that the Straight section in the clue is 'letters', which is a Double Meaning Word. Ground = LAND, ground = LORDS, which are two word exchanges.

I recommend that you try several newspapers to find one that suits you, as compilers do have their own particular style and gradually you will build up a rapport with them. Of course some newspapers use more than one compiler and you will eventually learn to detect this.

Every morning I buy 2 newspapers, one which I enjoy reading, the other purely for the crossword.

EPILOGUE

Many years ago, during my infant schooldays, I discovered a source of great pleasure which still today, 37 years on, is no less of a joy. My memories of those early years recall being given the opportunity to write on new, clean, ruled paper. But my favourite was Quadrille, *which was squared* and used for mathematics.

Requesting a new nib, I would proceed to write in my neatest handwriting. The enjoyment I got from writing on new paper totally overrode the anxiety suffered by classmates during exam times. Questions with *little boxes* that required *answers* and working in the silent conditions that were peculiar to the exam times — that pleasure remains with me still. After the purchase of my newspaper, it is neatly folded into a half then a quarter, leaving the cryptic crossword framed, and inviting to be solved.

In learning we have been friends; now that I am a compiler we are foes.
                                                                    K. Skinner